C

WRITERS ON FILE

General Editor: Simon Trussler

Associate Editor: Malcolm Page

D0714048

BECKETT
on File

Compiled by Virginia Cooke

Methuen. London and New York

First published in 1985 in
simultaneous hardback and paperback editions
by Methuen London Ltd,
11 New Fetter Lane, London EC4P 4EE
and Methuen Inc, 733 Third Avenue,
New York, NY 10017

Typeset in IBM 9pt Press Roman
by 🅵\ Tek-Art, Croydon, Surrey
Printed in Great Britain by
Hazell Watson & Viney Ltd
Member of the BPCC Group,
Aylesbury, Bucks.

British Library Cataloguing in Publication Data

Cooke, Virginia
    Beckett on file. — (Playwrights on file)
    1. Beckett, Samuel — Criticism and interpretation
    I. Title   II. Series
    822'.912   PR6003.E282Z/

    ISBN 0-413-58510-7
    ISBN 0-413-54560-1 Pbk

Cover image based on a photo by John Haynes

Contents

The theatre is, by its nature, an ephemeral art: yet it is a daunting task to track down the newspaper reviews, or contemporary statements from the writer or his director, which are often all that remain to help us recreate some sense of what a particular production was like. This series is therefore intended to make readily available a selection of the comments that the critics made about the plays of leading modern dramatists at the time of their production – and to trace, too, the course of each writer's own views about his work and his world.

In addition to combining a uniquely convenient source of such elusive *documentation*, the 'Writers on File' series also assembles the *information* necessary for readers to pursue further their interest in a particular writer or work. Variations in quantity between one writer's output and another, differences in temperament which make some readier than others to talk about their work, and the variety of critical response, all mean that the presentation and balance of material shifts between one volume and another: but we have tried to arrive at a format for the series which will nevertheless enable users of one volume readily to find their way around any other.

Section 1, 'A Brief Chronology', provides a quick conspective overview of each playwright's life and career. *Section 2* deals with the plays themselves, arranged chronologically in the order of their composition: information on first performances, major revivals, and publication is followed by a brief synopsis (for quick reference set in slightly larger, italic type), then by a representative selection of the critical response, and of the dramatist's own comments on the play and its theme.

Section 3 offers concise guidance to each writer's work in non-dramatic forms, while *Section 4,* 'The Writer on His Work', brings together comments from the playwright himself on more general matters of construction, opinion, and artistic development. Finally, *Section 5* provides a bibliographical guide to other primary and secondary sources of further reading, among which full details will be found of works cited elsewhere under short titles, and of collected editions of the plays – but not of individual titles, particulars of which will be found with the other factual data in Section 2.

In the case of Samuel Beckett, an author almost uniquely reluctant to discuss his work, the comments available from the writer are few indeed — though Beckett's increasing tendency to participate in the directing of his own plays, and to work regularly with particular actors and directors, means that on occasion his views may be deduced, albeit in reported or secondhand form.

The compiler has included such comments where they are available, and has also, of course, had to take into account that — in part *because* of Beckett's own silence, in part because of the nature of his plays — a great deal of the comment available is of an interpretive, literary-critical kind, and so treats the plays as textual problems to be solved rather than as scenarios for live performance. The best of such criticism is listed in the bibliography of secondary literature, but in her choice of extracts for the volume itself Ms Cooke has rightly sought out those responses which illuminate the plays as vehicles for actors, not puzzles for scholars.

Beckett is also unusual among modern dramatists in that he turned to the theatre relatively late in his creative career. A particular feature of this volume is thus the attention given both to his output of novels, and also to the various, surprisingly successful attempts to adapt his prose works for stage performance.

More typically, at least among those writers represented so far in the present series, Beckett tends to be well known for a relatively small proportion of his total output. Such plays as *Waiting for Godot, Endgame,* and *Happy Days* are widely-recognized classics of the modern repertoire, yet some of his work remains virtually unknown — not so much because of changes in his own artistic position or of theatrical fashion, as because of the increasingly stringent process of artistic filtration to which he has subjected his material. Thus, while the better-known plays, however baffling early critics found them, were nevertheless of that 'certain length' which theatregoers have recognized since the days of Aeschylus, much of his later work has been almost imagist in its compression of experience.

In presenting here what may be for many readers a first acquaintance with such plays, it is hoped, therefore, that the interest of these pieces may be more widely recognized. Though they refuse to fit the straitjacket of managerial preconceptions, they can often be extraordinarily rewarding — not least for students or actors in training who wish to test to the limit the potential of the theatrical experience, and of their own skills.

Simon Trussler

1906 13 Apr. (Good Friday) is the date usually given for Samuel Barclay Beckett's birth, but the birth certificate shows 13 May. He was born in the family home of Cooldrinagh in Foxrock, south of Dublin, to William Beckett, surveyor, and Mary (May) Roe, daughter of a wealthy Kildare family. 'You might say I had a happy childhood ... My father did not beat me, nor did my mother run away from home' (Beckett, quoted in Dierdre Bair, *Samuel Beckett*, p. 22).

1911-19 Beckett and his older brother Frank attended first the private academy of Miss Ida Elsnor, then Earlsfort House School, Dublin.

1920 Sent to Portora Royal School in Eniskillan, Northern Ireland, where he excelled more in sports than studies as star bowler on the cricket team, captain of rugby and swimming, and light-heavyweight champion in boxing.

1923 Entered Trinity College, Dublin, studying Modern Languages under Dr. Rudmose-Brown, but continuing to play cricket and golf. He developed a taste for the theatre of Pirandello and O'Casey, variety, and the cinema of Charlie Chaplin, Laurel and Hardy, and the Marx Brothers (Bair, p.50).

1927 8 Dec., received his BA degree, first in his class in modern languages.

1928-30 Became a *lecteur* at the École Normale Superieure in Paris, where he met James Joyce, who profoundly influenced him. Besides aiding Joyce in various ways, Beckett wrote an essay, 'Dante ... Bruno. Vico ... Joyce', and his first short story, 'Assumption'. He studied Descartes, translated Italian poetry for Samuel Putnam, and began writing poetry. 15 June 1930, *Whoroscope* published by Hours Press. Also in 1930, wrote the critical volume *Proust*.

1930-32 Returned to Dublin to teach French at Trinity College, and became a close friend of Jack B. Yeats. For Trinity College's annual drama festival, he created *Le Kid*, a parody of Corneille's *Le Cid*. He wrote poems, translations, and part of *Dream of Fair to Middling Women*, a novel never finished. Dec. 1931, resigned his teaching post to return first to Germany, then to Paris.

1: A Brief Chronology

1932 The prose pieces, 'Sedendo et Queenscendo' and 'Text' published in Paris. He returned, jobless and penniless, to Dublin.

1933-34 Wrote seven stories, six of which were later included in *More Pricks than Kicks*. He nursed his father through recovery from a heart attack, but a second attack on 26 June killed William Beckett. Dec., moved to London and began psychoanalysis at the Tavistock Clinic. 24 May 1934, *More Pricks than Kicks* published, but Beckett turned to literary criticism to eke out a meagre living.

1935-38 Wrote the novel *Murphy,* and the poem 'Cascando'. Having helped Mrs. Mary Manning Howe revise a play, he began to attend rehearsals at the Peacock and old Abbey Theatres, and toyed with writing a play about Samuel Johnson. In 1937 he returned to Paris: 'I didn't like living in Ireland. You know the kind of thing – theocracy, censorship of books. . . . I preferred to live abroad' (letter to Thomas McGreevy, quoted by Bair, p.230). Finally in 1937, after 42 rejections, Routledge agreed to publish *Murphy*.

1938-43 Met Suzanne Dechevaux-Dumesnil, who became his companion and eventually his wife. He began writing poems in French (published as a cycle in 1946). Beckett and Suzanne became active in the French Resistance, and by 1942 had to flee from Paris to Roussillon, where they lived in hiding until 1944.

1943-45 Still hiding in exile, wrote the novel *Watt*. At the war's end, he returned briefly to Dublin, then joined an Irish Red Cross medical unit which was setting up a hospital in France. 30 Mar. 1945, awarded the Croix de Guerre and the Medaille de la Resistance.

1946-48 Beckett wrote critical essays, the short stories 'La Fin' and 'Suite', and began *Mercier et Camier*, his first novel in French. Oct. 1946, wrote 'L'Expulse' and 'Premier Amour' (not published until 1970). In 1947 he wrote his first play *Eleutheria*, and half finished the novel *Molloy*, followed by its sequel, *Malone meurt*. Again, he had trouble finding a publisher.

1949-50 Jan., finished *En Attendant Godot* 'as a relaxation, to get away from the awful prose I was writing at the time' (Bair, p.581). He continued to translate for Duthuit's *Transition*, for which he also wrote an article about modern art called 'Three Dialogues'. Began *L'Innommable*. Impressed with Roger Blin's production of Strindberg's *Ghost Sonata*, Beckett left his manuscripts of *Eleutheria* and *Godot* with Blin for possible production.

1950-52 25 Aug. 1950, May Beckett died (and, with her, Beckett's last strong connection with Ireland). Jerome Lindon accepted

Beckett's trilogy, *Molloy*, *Malone meurt*, and *L'Innommable*. UNESCO commissioned a translation of 35 Mexican poets. In 1951 *En Attendant Godot* was published by Minuit, and in 1952 Roger Blin received a grant to subsidize the production of *Godot*, part of the play being broadcast on French radio in Feb. Beckett and Suzanne bought a plot of land in Ussy and built a small house, which became his refuge from an increasingly hectic life in Paris and often the only place he could write.

1953 5 Jan., *En Attendant Godot* premiered in Paris at the Théâtre de Babylone, without Beckett's attendance. *Watt* published by the magazine *Merlin*. Beckett wrote pieces of short prose, later collected in *Textes pour rien* (published in 1955), and began translating his work into English. Characteristically involved in the production of his plays, he oversaw rehearsals of *Godot* in Germany and Paris.

1954-55 Wrote *Fin de partie,* 3 Aug. 1955, after continuous battles with the Lord Chamberlain over the language, Peter Hall's production of *Waiting for Godot* opened in London. In Paris, Beckett created *Acte sans paroles I*, a skit for dancer Deryk Mendel.

1956 Jan., Alan Schneider directed the American premiere of *Godot* in Miami, where it met with a hostile audience, but reopened successfully in New York, 19 Apr. From Paris Beckett comforted the distressed Schneider with the comment: 'Success and failure on the public level never mattered much to me, in fact I feel much more at home with the latter, having breathed deep of its vivifying air all my writing life up to the last couple of years' ('Beckett's Letters on *Endgame*,' in *The Village Voice Reader*, p. 183). June, Trinity College published *From an Abandoned Work*. Sept., Beckett wrote *All that Fall*, a radio play transmitted by the BBC on 13 Jan. 1957.

1957 Minuit published *Fin de partie* and *Acte sans paroles*. Robert Pinget's translation of *All That Fall* published as *Toux ce qui tombent*. 28 Mar., Jack Yeats died, and Beckett wrote, 'The light of Jack Yeats will always come with me' (letter to H.O. White, quoted by Bair, p.408). 3 Apr., *Fin de partie* opened at the Royal Court Theatre to negative reviews, and at the Champs Élysées in Paris on 27 Apr.

1958 28 Oct., Royal Court staged the English version, *Endgame*. Beckett began *Krapps' Last Tape* for actor Patrick Magee; along with *Endgame*, it opened in London in Oct. Translated *L'Innommable* into English.

1959 25 Feb., Beckett awarded an honorary doctorate from Trinity College. From the citation: 'Perhaps it is not an unjustifiable comparison to recall how in ancient Greece the philosopher Diogenes ... exercised his mordant wit and vivid symbolism against the follies and vices of the age. But this our modern Diogenes shows a greater compassion and humanity when he brings out weaknesses into the light of truth.' Mar., his translation of *Krapp's Last Tape* published. Collaborated with Marcel Mihalovici in the operatic version, *Das letze Band,* translated into German by Elmar Tophoven.

1959-60 Beckett worked on *Comment C'est,* published in 1961. Sept. 1959, *Embers* won the Prix Italia. *La Dernière Bande,* translated by Beckett and Pierre Leyris, published in Paris, 1960, and performed 22 Mar. at Théâtre Recamier, Paris.

1961 *Comment C'est* published in Paris, and *Poems in English* in London. 25 Mar., Beckett and Suzanne married in Bristol. He finished *Happy Days,* and shared the Prix International des Editeurs with Jorge Louis Borges. 13 Sept., *Happy Days* premiered in New York under Alan Schneider's direction, and opened in Germany, 30 Sept. Wrote *Words and Music.*

1962 1 Nov., *Happy Days* opened at the Royal Court, London; *Words and Music* broadcast by BBC, 13 Nov. Beckett wrote the radio play *Cascando,* worked on *Play,* and, with Jack MacGowran, on a one-man show, *End of Day,* which opened at the Gaiety Theatre, Dublin, 5 Oct.

1963 Beckett worked on French and German translations of *Play,* which premiered in Ulm Donau, 16 June.

1964 4 Jan., *Play* opened in New York, and on 11 June the French translation, *Comédie,* performed in Paris. July, Beckett went to New York to oversee the shooting of *Film,* directed by Alan Schneider and starring Buster Keaton; this won the New York Film Festival Award, the Diploma de Merito in Venice, and the 'outstanding film' award at the London Film Festival (1965). 6 Oct., *Cascando* broadcast by BBC. Beckett wrote *Eh Joe,* a television play, and *Come and Go,* translated as *Va et vient.*

1965-68 Beckett translated *Eh Joe (Dis Joe),* along with *Paroles et musique. Come and Go* performed at the Schiller Theatre, Berlin. *Imagination morte imaginez* published in Oct. 1965 in Paris, and in Nov. *Imagination Dead Imagine* in London. 28 Feb. 1966, *Va et vient* produced at Odéon-Théâtre, Paris, 8 Mar. 1966, *Poems I* compiled and narrated on BBC. *Play* filmed in Paris.

Beckett directed productions of *Eh Joe* in Stuttgart and London. 3 Oct. 1966, *Comédie* opened at the Odéon. The prose texts of *Ping* and *Assez* were published by Minuit. 25 Sept. 1967, Beckett directed *Endgame* at the Schiller Theater in Berlin. 28 Feb. 1968, first English production of *Come and Go* at Peacock Theatre, Dublin.

1969 *Sans* published in Paris. 23 Oct., Beckett awarded the Nobel Prize for Literature for 'a body of work that, in new forms of fiction and the theatre, has transmuted the destitution of modern man into his exaltation'. This resulted in the appearance of previously unpublished works and plans for a Samuel Beckett Theatre at Oxford. 15 Oct., Beckett underwent successful operation for glaucoma after suffering greatly with his eyes.

1970 *Lessness* (Beckett's translation of *Sans*), *Mercier et Camier*, 'Premier Amour', and Le Dépeupleur' published.

1971 Directed *Happy Days* (*Glükliche Tage*) at the Schiller Theater for the Berlin Festival.

1972-74 Wrote two plays, *Not I* and *That Time,* as well as some short prose works. 22 Nov, 1972, *Not I* premiered at the Lincoln Centre in New York, as part of a two-part Beckett festival arranged by Hume Cronyn, Jessica Tandy, and Alan Schneider. 16 Jan. 1973, Beckett assisted with the London production of *Not I* at the Royal Court. Worked on translations and publication of previous works, much in demand since his Nobel Prize.

1975-77 Beckett directed *Waiting for Godot* at the Schiller Theater. *Pas Moi* (the French version of *Not I*) opened at the Petit Théâtre d'Orsay, Paris. May 1976, the Royal Court staged a Seventieth Birthday Season in honour of Beckett, which included productions of *Waiting for Godot* (in German, with the Schiller company which Beckett had directed), *Endgame, Play,* and two new works, *That Time* and *Footfalls.* Dec. 1976, *Play, That Time,* and *Footfalls* produced in Washington, D.C. These plays, along with *Ghost Trio,* a television play, published in *Ends and Odds.* 17 Apr. 1977, *Ghost Trio* and '. . . but the clouds . . . ' performed on BBC Television.

1978-80 In 1978 Minuit published *Mirlitonnades,* 35 short poems written in French between 1976 and 1978. *A Piece of Monologue,* written in 1979 and published in *The Kenyon Review,* performed in New York by David Warrilow. Beckett wrote *Company,* a prose text, first in French and then in English. 'One Evening', translated from the French, published.

11

1981 Beckett wrote *Mal vu mal dit* and the English version, *Ill Seen Ill Said.* 8 Apr., *Rockaby* (written in 1980) premiered at a Beckett Festival held at the Centre for Research in Buffalo, New York. 9 May, Alan Schneider directed this as well as *Ohio Impromptu,* written for a Beckett conference at Ohio State University: both published by Grove Press. Beckett wrote *Catastrophe,* dedicated to the imprisoned Czech dramatist Vaclav Havel.

1982 *Catastrophe* first performed at the Avignon Theatre Festival. Dec., *Rockaby* played at the Cottesloe Theatre, London, accompanied by Billie Whitelaw's reading of the short story, *Enough,* and BBC Television presented a week-long Beckett season, featuring *Happy Days, Not I, Eh Joe, Rockaby,* and *Quad.*

1983 10 Jan., English translation of *Catastrophe* printed in *The New Yorker.* June, *Catastrophe,* along with *Ohio Impromptu* and *What Where,* opened under Alan Schneider's direction at the Harold Clurman Theatre, New York. In London John Calder published *Disjecta,* a collection of short prose pieces and a dramatic fragment previously 'unpublished or published obscurely'; and *Collected Shorter Plays,* a valuable edition of 29 short plays from *All That Fall* to *What Where,* published by Faber and Faber.

1984 Beckett arrived in New York to direct the San Quentin Drama Group's *Waiting for Godot.*

Waiting for Godot

Play in two acts.

Written: in French, as *En Attendant Godot*, 1949; *translated* into English by Beckett.

First Paris production: Théâtre de Babylone, 5 Jan. 1953 (dir. Roger Blin).

First London production: Art Th. Club, 3 Aug. 1955 (dir. Peter Hall).

First American production: Coconut Grove Playhouse, Miami, 3 Jan. 1956 (dir. Alan Schneider).

Revived: John Golden Th., New York, 19 Apr. 1956 (dir. Herbert Berghof); Theatre Hébertôt, Paris, June 1956; at San Quentin, 19 Nov. 1957; first unexpurgated version, Royal Court Th., 30 Dec.1964 (dir. Anthony Page, supervised by Beckett); Schiller Th., Berlin, Apr. 1975 (dir. Beckett), in German; Arena Th., Washington, D.C., Dec. 1976 (dir. Alan Schneider); Citizens Th., Glasgow, Apr. 1982 (by an all-female cast).

Published: Paris: Éditions de minuit, 1952; New York: Grove Press, 1954; London: Faber and Faber, 1956.

Vladimir (Didi) and Estragon (Gogo), two tramps, are discovered on a lonely road, awaiting the arrival of someone named Godot. While they wait, they banter, argue, engage in comic business reminiscent of vaudeville or silent comic films, and try to establish whether this is the spot and time at which they have been directed to wait. Two more men arrive: tyrannical Pozzo, whom at first Didi and Gogo mistake for Godot, and his slave, Lucky, who is made to dance and to 'think' for their entertainment. After Pozzo and Lucky depart, a small boy appears to announce that Godot cannot make it after all, but that he will surely come 'tomorrow'. The curtain falls as the two tramps contemplate suicide. Act Two opens on the same scene, but the bare tree of Act One has sprouted a few leaves. Still Didi and Gogo wait, again distracted by Lucky (now dumb) and Pozzo (now blind). They leave. Again the boy arrives with a message from Godot. The tramps say they'll leave, but they go on waiting with a mixture of hope and fear.

[Beckett has consistently declined to elucidate the meaning of Godot, as he has eschewed commentary on all his works. He did comment that 'if you want to find the origins of *Waiting for Godot*, look at *Murphy*' (Colin Duckworth, 'The Making of *Godot*', in *Casebook on Waiting for Godot*, p. 89). Beckett was present at every rehearsal of the original French production, and became as important as Roger Blin in the direction of the play; he has taken a major part in many of the subsequent productions.]

I plied [Beckett] with all my studiously-arrived-at questions . . . and he tried to answer as directly and honestly as he could. The first one was 'Who or what does Godot mean?' and the answer was immediately forthcoming: 'If I knew, I would have said so in the play'.
Alan Schneider, *Chelsea Review,* September 1958, p. 8,
reprinted in *Casebook,* p. 55

But when the curtain fell, and they heard the enthusiasm of the audience, they understood at least this much: Paris had just recognized in Samuel Beckett one of today's best playwrights . . . These two tramps, who represent all humanity, utter remarks that any one of us might utter. These two men are feeble and energetic, cowardly and courageous; they bicker, amuse themselves, are bored, speak to each other without understanding. They do all this to keep busy. To pass time. To live or to give themselves the illusion that they are living.
Sylvain Zegal, *Libération*, 7 Jan. 1953, trans.
Ruby Cohn in *Critical Heritage,* p.88

The extraordinary success of Samuel Beckett is primarily due to the artistry with which he gives life and presence to this waiting — we know what it represents. We do it too, we participate in it completely. . . . A profoundly original work; because of this it will necessarily be a disconcerting one. Either it will charm the public or arouse contempt, even fury.
Jacques Lemarchand, *Figaro Littéraire,* 17 Jan. 1953, p.10 trans.
Jean M. Sommermeyer in *Critical Heritage*, p.91

The objections to Mr. Samuel Beckett's play as theatrical entertainment are many and obvious. . . . In the course of the play, nothing happens. Such dramatic progress as there is, is not towards a climax, but towards a perpetual postponement. . . . The dialogue is studded with words that have no meaning for normal ears.

... The upshot of *Waiting for Godot* is that the two tramps are always waiting for the future, their ruinous consolations being that there is always tomorrow; they never realize that today is today. In this, says Mr. Beckett, they are like humanity, which dawdles and drivels away its life ... at the worst you will discover a curiosity, a four-leaved clover, a black tulip; at the best, something that will securely lodge in a corner of your mind for as long as you live.

Harold Hobson, *Sunday Times,* 7 Aug. 1955, p.11

A play, it asserts and proves, is basically a means of spending two hours in the dark without being bored. ... The play sees the human condition in terms of baggy pants and red noses. ... It summoned the music hall and the parable to present a view of life which banished the sentimentality of the music hall and the parable's fulsome uplift. It forced me to re-examine the rules which have hitherto governed the drama; and, having done so, to pronounce them not elastic enough.

Kenneth Tynan, *The Observer,* 7 Aug. 1955, p. 11, reprinted in
A View of the English Stage (London: Davis-Poynter, 1975),
p.158-61

It is not Pascal at all, but rather Joyce who holds the reins. The freedom of language, its disorder, its calculated follies, and this prodigious equilibrium of words are all derived from Joyce. The battering ram of philosophy used to force open the gate of a melancholy philosophy ... nausea rises, malaise remains. This malaise, as in all of Beckett's plays, is due to a sort of passion for the morbid, for decay, for the ruin of flesh and brains. ... With Beckett, theatre is already in its grave.

Pierre Marcabru, *Arts Spectacles,* 10-16 May 1961, p.14, trans.
Jean M. Sommermeyer in *Critical Heritage,* p.115

Two men waiting, for another whom they know only by an implausible name which may not be his real name. A ravaged and blasted landscape. A world that was ampler and more open once, but is permeated with pointlessness now. Mysterious dispensers of beatings. A man of property and his servant, in flight. And the anxiety of the two who wait, their anxiety to be as inconspicuous as possible in a strange environment ... where their mere presence is likely to cause remark. It is curious how readers and audiences

15

do not think to observe the most obvious thing about the world of this play, that it resembles France occupied by the Germans, in which its author spent the war years. How much waiting must have gone on in that bleak world; how many times must Resistance operatives ... have kept appointments not knowing whom they were to meet. ... We can easily see why a Pozzo would be un-nerving. ... He may be a Gestapo official clumsily disguised. Here is perhaps the playwright's most remarkable feat. There existed, throughout a whole country for five years, a literal situation that corresponded point by point with the situation in this play, and was so far from special that millions of lives were saturated in its desperate reagents, and no spectator ever thinks of it.

Hugh Kenner, *Reader's Guide,* p.30

The seed of *Godot* is Luke's account of the crucifixion, as sum-marized by St. Augustine: 'Do not despair: one of the thieves was saved. Do not presume: one of the thieves was damned.' The two thieves are Didi and Gogo; the two thieves are Pozzo and Lucky; the two thieves are you and me. And the play is shaped to reflect that fearful symmetry.

Ruby Cohen, *Back to Beckett,* p.13

His English title does not translate the much more apt French one ... which means '*while* waiting for Godot'. The subject is not of pure waiting. It is: what happens in certain human beings *while* waiting. In waiting they show, ultimately, human dignity: they have kept their appointment, even if Godot has not.

Eric Bentley, 'Postscript 1967', *New Republic,*
reprinted in *Critical Heritage*, p.110

All That Fall

Radio play in one act.
Written: in English, 1956; *translated* into French as *Tous ceux qui tombent* by Beckett and Roger Pinget.
First production: BBC Third Programme, 13 Jan. 1957 (dir. Donald McWhinnie).
Stage production: in German, Schiller Th., Werkstatt, Berlin, Jan. 1966.
Published: New York: Grove Press; London: Faber and Faber, 1957; Paris: Éditions de minuit, 1957.

Set in rural Ireland, All That Fall *is essentially the story of Maddy Roony's trip to the railway station to meet her blind husband and walk him home. Aged and immensely overweight, Mrs. Rooney sweats and puffs and labours her way along, encountering a cart man, a man on a bicycle, and another man who gives her a lift in his car. We learn that she has lost her daughter ('Little Minnie'); the trouble, her doctor had declared, 'was that she had never been really born.' Mr. Rooney's train is late because of some mysterious mishap. In their conversation on the way home, Mr. Rooney seems dry and unfeeling and on a final ironic note we learn the reason for the train's delay: a child has fallen under the wheels and been killed.*

Never thought about a radio play technique . . . but in the dead of t'other night got a nice gruesome idea full of cartwheels and dragging feet and puffing and panting which may or may not lead to something.

Beckett, letter to Nancy Cunard, 5 July 1956,
quoted by Bair, p. 401

What raises this play, also, above the mere desolating wit of *Fin de partie* is the Irish love of extravagant language that runs through it. . . . There is a warmth in the incidental humour, though it may be unintended warmth. . . . This is a play by a man at the end of his tether; but that tether, tying Mr. Beckett, perhaps reluctantly, to sympathy with those who fall and those who are bowed down, has not yet been broken.

Times Literary Supplement, 6 Sept. 1957, p.528,
reprinted in *Critical Heritage,* p.153

[Mrs. Rooney] speaks by formula, but she does not live and feel by formula – or she strives not to, though her language continually traps her into it. . . . A concern with the dignity or the decrepitude of language is, after all, a concern for the dignity or decrepitude of man. To the writer of the twentieth century who, like his contemporaries the painters and sculptors, disdains to do anything with his art more questionable than explore the nature of his own medium, words in arrangements, the question of human dignity cannot present itself in any other terms than those of the dignity of human language. . . . And Beckett, when he is not stooping to trick-endings and symbolic puns, is of those modern writers who have withdrawn into a sheerly verbal universe, not in order to exclude the more troublous worlds of experience, but precisely to see all those wider troubles at work in language as in a microcosm.

Donald Davie, *Spectrum,* Winter 1958, p .29,
reprinted in *Critical Heritage,* p. 158

Their gloom . . . is so excessive that Beckett milks it cannily — at least at the beginning of the play — for pure comedy. Mrs. Rooney is made into one of those women whose only satisfaction is in the sickness, operations, and bereavements they have endured. Her keening is continually parodied both by her own soap-opera and also by the sounds of an irrepressible nature . . . a nature made deliberately intrusive by courtesy of the Special Effects Department. . . . It is as though the cast of *Murphy* had suddenly appeared in the closing pages of the trilogy (which, in turn, is like casting the Marx Brothers in a play by Eugene O'Neill).

A. Alvarez, *Beckett,* p. 113-14

All That Fall . . . ends ambiguously according to daytime logic but logically according to the laws of a world where all reality is audible. Dan Rooney has pondered how it would be to murder a child . . . and his train came in late because a child, as we learn, slipped down under the wheels, and yet it seems meaningless to ask whether he pushed her there; for the very journey, since it occupies no air-time, is sheer illusion conjured up for us by his telling of what he chooses to tell, a telling according to which he did nothing at all except experience bladder distress. . . . Knowing how dependent we should be on words, Beckett in his first radio script lavished all his resources of eloquence on shaping the speeches; the work may have relieved him amid *Endgame*'s austerities. And since sound passes even as we hear it, in *All That Fall* all passes, dwindles, falls, as transient as breath.

Hugh Kenner, *Reader's Guide*, p. 159-60

Endgame

Play in one act.
Written: in French, as *Fin de partie,* 1954-56; *translated* into English by Beckett.
First London production: in French, Royal Court Th., 3 Apr. 1957 (dir. Roger Blin).

First Paris production: Studio des Champs Élysées, 26 Apr. 1957.
First American production: Cherry Lane Th., New York, 28 Jan.
   1958 (dir. Alan Schneider).
First English production of English translation, Royal Court Th.,
   28 Oct. 1958 (dir. George Devine).
Revived: BBC Radio, 22 May 1962; Aldwych Th., by the Royal
   Shakespeare Co., 9 July 1964; Schiller Th., Berlin 25 Sept.
   1967 (dir. Beckett); Manhattan Project, New York, 7 Feb. 1973
   (dir. Andre Gregory); Royal Court Th., London, as part of the
   Beckett Festival, 6 May 1976 (dir. Donald McWhinnie); Young
   Vic, London, 29 Jan. 1980 (dir. Beckett); Goodman Th.,
   Chicago, by the San Quentin Workshop, 27 Sept., 1980
   (dir. Beckett);
Published: Paris: Éditions de minuit, 1957; New York: Grove
   Press; London: Faber and Faber, 1958.

*Set in a bleak room with two small windows looking out onto
an almost lifeless world,* Endgame *provides a stage picture of T.S.
Eliot's last lines from 'The Hollow Men': 'This is the way the
world ends/Not with a bang but with a whimper'. The blind
character Hamm rules this diminished universe from his centre-
stage wheelchair, as he barks his orders to Clov, who resentfully
follows every order – moving the chair, checking the earth and
sky, supplying pain-killers and time-killers. The only other characters are Hamm's parents, Nagg and Nell – or what is left of
them, for, without legs or pulse, they are stationed side-by-side
in dustbins, occasionally providing memories of life and love.
Clov's opening lines set the tone: 'Finished, it's nearly finished,
it must be nearly finished', followed by Hamm's 'And yet I
hesitate, I hesitate to . . . end'. Their exchanges, despairing but
often comic, fill the time until Clov, dressed to leave but with
nowhere to go, stands motionless by the door as Hamm awaits
the end. 'Do you believe in the life to come?' asks Clov at one
point, to which Hamm replies, 'Mine was always that'.*

Beckett's most explicit [statement about *Fin de partie*] came
when Beckett directed his own production in Berlin in 1967. To
Hamm played by Ernst Schroder, Beckett explained: '[Hamm]
is a king in the chess game lost from the start. From the start he
knows he is making loud senseless moves. That he will make no

19

progress at all with the gaff. Now at the last he makes a few senseless moves as only a bad player would. A good one would have given up long ago. He is only trying to delay the inevitable end. Each of his gestures is one of the last useless moves which put off the end. He's a bad player.'

Ruby Cohn, *Back to Beckett*, p. 152.

But when it comes to journalists, I feel the only line is to refuse to be involved in exegesis of any kind. And to insist on the extreme simplicity of dramatic situation and issue. If that's not enough for them, and it obviously isn't, it's plenty for us, and we have no elucidations to offer of mysteries that are all of their making. My work is a matter of fundamental sounds (no joke intended) made as fully as possible, and I accept responsibility for nothing else. If people want to have headaches among the overtones, let them. And provide their own aspirin. Hamm as stated, and Clov as stated, *nec tecum nec sine te,* in such a place, and in such a world, that's all I can manage, more than I could.

Beckett, letter to Alan Schneider, 29 Dec. 1957, quoted in
Village Voice Reader, p. 185, and reprinted in *Disjecta,* p. 109

Generally speaking, a chess game has three parts: first is the opening, in which pieces are brought out and strategies instigated. In the next section, or middle game, the two opponents organize their moves. In the last part, the endgame . . . there are no longer enough pieces left on the board to initiate an attack upon the king. This is when both kings are free to come to the centre of the board, to confront each other, seemingly uncaring, as they execute the few limited moves still possible.

Dierdre Bair, *Samuel Beckett,* p. 394

Mr. Beckett is a poet; and the business of a poet is not to clarify, but to suggest, to imply, to employ words with auras of association, with a reaching out towards a vision, a probing down into emotion, beyond the compass of explicit definition. And this is exactly what the so dangerously simple dialogue of *Fin de partie* does.

Harold Hobson, *Sunday Times,* 7 Apr. 1957, p. 15

The play is an allegory about authority, an attempt to dramatize the neurosis that makes men love power. The new play, directed by Roger Blin under the author's supervision, makes it clear that his purpose is neither to move us nor to help us. For him, man is a pygmy who connives at his own horrible degradation. There says Beckett, stamping on the face of mankind: there, that is how life is.

Kenneth Tynan, *The Observer,* 7 Apr. 1957, p. 15

The humour of this grim play — vigorous, savage, never gratuitous, provoking brusque outbreaks of laughter — arises also from flashes of confrontation between the actual situation of these characters and the tremendous futility of their malice as well as their moments of tenderness. It arises too from the frenzy we discover in these characters, which they reveal in their furious acceptance of their fate.... Black humour indeed, but of a kind that arises spontaneously from felicitous and unexpected phrases, from a latent tragicomicality that suddenly becomes enormously ludicrous.

Jacques Lemarchand, *Figaro Littéraire,* 11 May 1957, p. 14, trans. Jean M. Sommermeyer in *Critical Heritage,* p. 170

If he [Rick Cluchey of the San Quentin Workshop] achieves Beckett's vision of *Endgame* it will appear as a comic sonata about the end of the world, musical, lyrical, dark....

Ned Chaillet, *The Times,* 28 July 1980, p. 11

Endgame is constructed in more or less clearly defined sections which are 'played without a break'; the sections being frequently marked off by pauses but never by an interval as significant as that between the movements in a piece of music. Hamm and Clov correspond constructionally less to the 'characters' in a traditional play than to musical instruments. Their special characteristics are not used in the development of a plot, but to carry as it were pitch and timbre, to give off matching or dissonant tones and colours. If we think of Hamm and Clov in the first instance as, for example, cello and violin instead of two people that we might see walking the streets; if we think of Nell and Nagg as, say, a pair of flutes; we are already closer to understanding the construction of the play.

John Fletcher and John Spurling, *Beckett: a Study of His Plays,* p. 72

Act without Words I

Mime for one player.
Written: in French as *Acte sans paroles,* 1956.
First London production: Royal Court Th., as an afterpiece to
Fin de partie, 3 Apr. 1957 (dir. and performed by Deryk
Mendel; music John Beckett).
Revived: In-Stage Th., London, July 1962; Telfis Eireann, May
1963; Lincoln Centre, New York, at the Beckett Festival,
Nov. 1970.
Published: Paris: Editions de minuit, 1957, with *Fin de partie;*
New York: Grove Press, with *Endgame,* 1958.

*Set in the desert in 'blinding light', Act without Words captures
the futility of man's efforts. The clownish mimer is 'flung' on the
stage and flung back on twice as he tries to leave. Forced to stay
in this desert, he is then tantalized with objects which might offer
some comfort – a shady tree and a pitcher of water. But these are
controlled by some invisible outside source, and they are either
placed out of reach or else arbitrarily removed. Whistles from
above alert the man to the objects and to ropes or cubes which he
might use to reach them, but each of his renewed efforts is
thwarted; either he falls, or the object is raised just as he nearly
touches it. Finally, the man's conditioning is complete: he no
longer responds to the whistle or the promises from above.*

The two *Acts without Words* seem to be loosely based on punish-
ments from the classical underworld: the first one that of
Tantalus, who was condemned to stand in a stream which receded
whenever he bent down to drink, while fruit-laden branches over-
head whisked out of his reach. . . . But *Act without Words I* is . . .
over-explicit, over-emphasized, and even, unless redeemed by its
performer, so unparticularized as to verge on the banal.

Fletcher and Spurling, *Beckett,* p. 119

Here Man (Deryk Mendel) is a shuffling puppet, obedient to the
imperious blasts of a whistle which send him vainly clambering
after a flask of water, lowered from above only to be whisked out
of reach. He is foiled even when he tries to hang himself, and ends
up inert, unresponsive to whistle and carafe alike. This kind of
facile pessimism is dismaying in an author of Beckett's stature.

It is not only the projection of a personal sickness, but a conclusion reached on inadequate evidence. I am ready to believe that the world is a stifling, constricting place — but not if my informant is an Egyptian mummy.

Kenneth Tynan, *The Observer*, 7 Apr. 1957, p. 15

Krapp's Last Tape

Play in one act.

Written: in English, 1957; *translated* into French as *La Dernière bande* by Beckett and Pierre Leyris.

First London production: Royal Court Th., 28 Oct. 1958 (dir. Donald McWhinnie).

First American production: Provincetown Playhouse, New York, 14 Jan. 1960 (dir. Alan Schneider).

First Paris production: Théâtre Récamier, 22 Mar. 1960 (dir. Roger Blin).

Revived: BBC Television, Nov. 1963; Schiller Th., Berlin, 5 Oct. 1969 (dir. Beckett); Petit Théâtre d'Orsay, Paris, April 1975 (dir. Beckett); Greenwich Th., London, in French, 8 Mar. 1976 (dir. Beckett); Goodman Studio Th., Chicago, by San Quentin Workshop 27 Sept. 1980 (dir. Beckett); BBC Television, Dec. 1982 (dir. Beckett). In March 1959, Marcel Mihilovici, with Beckett's collaboration, used *La Dernière bande* as the libretto for an opera.

Published: London: Faber and Faber, 1959, New York, Grove Press, 1960; Paris: Éditions de minuit, 1960.

Written for Patrick Magee, Krapp's Last Tape *stars a tape recorder featuring the voice of Krapp at the age of 39 and the listener, Krapp, at the age of 69, with 'cracked voice' and 'laborious walk'. The old man shuffles, eats bananas, drinks backstage, but above all listens intently and comments on his thoughts of thirty years ago. His chief fascination is with the memory of a night on a lake with a woman; twice he rewinds the reel in order to recapture the account. Then old Krapp puts on a new reel to record the present: 'Just been listening to that stupid bastard I took myself for thirty years ago, hard to believe I was ever as bad as that'. But he finds the current recording unsatisfactory, and returns again to his memories. The past and present are brought painfully together as Krapp regards his former self with disdain: 'All that old misery. Once wasn't enough for you.'*

23

It is one of the most openly autobiographical of his writings, and one which he worked over with painstaking precision in an attempt to disguise these traces. ... For the first time, he wrote about his mother's death.... Even Cissie Sinclair appears here called by her other nickname, 'Fanny'.

Dierdre Bair, *Samuel Beckett,* p. 415

Reduced to his most elementary appetites, Krapp has no purpose or occupation except to listen to his organs die and feel his functions fail. He is, like Eliot's Gerontion, 'an old man in a draughty house under a windy knob' but he is without even Gerontion's dream of rain.

Robert Brustein, *New Republic,* 22 Feb. 1960, p.21,
reprinted in *Seasons of Discontent* (New York:
Simon and Schuster, 1965), p. 26-8

SECK: Tuesday night, seven-thirty by the paranoid barometer, curtain up at the Court, Sam Beckett unrivalled master of the unravelled revels. Item: *Krapp's Last Tape,* Krapp being a myopic not to say deaf not to say eremitical eater of one and one-half bananas listening and cackling as he listens to a tape recording of twenty years' antiquity made on a day, the one far gone day when he laid his hand on a girl in a boat and it worked, as it worked for Molly Bloom in Gibraltar in the long ago. Actor: Patrick Magee, bereaved and aghast-looking grunting into his Grundig, probably perfect performance, fine throughout and highly affecting at the curtain-call though not formerly. Unique, oblique, bleak experience, in other words, and would have had same effect if half the words were other word. Or any words. *(Pause).*

SLAMM: Don't stop. You're boring me.

SECK *(normal voice):* Not enough. You're smiling.

SLAMM: Well, I'm still in the land of the dying.

SECK: Somehow, in spite of everything, death goes on . . .

SLAMM: Is that all the review he's getting?

SECK: That's all the play he's written.

SLAMM: But a genius. Could you do as much?

SECK: Not as much. But as little.

Kenneth Tynan, *'Slamm's Last Knock,* a play inspired, if that is the word, by Samuel Beckett's double bill at the Royal Court'
The Observer, 2 Nov. 1958, p. 19,
reprinted in *A View of the English Stage,* p.232-5

The tape recorder becomes Krapp's time machine, transporting him back, while we compare three Krapps at once, each addicted to bananas ... each prey to women and alcohol; each desperate to dam time's unbearable flow with language.

Elin Diamond, *Theatre Journal,* XXXII (Mar. 1981)

[Krapp] has been unmoved, except to the occasional 'brief laugh' by his *doppelgänger's* earlier reminiscences, but it is a measure of how much this play needs to be experienced in the theatre, rather than simply read, that these double laughs — the laughs of middle-aged Krapp on the tape, accompanied by the laughs of old Krapp on the stage, culminating in a laugh by the old Krapp which is not shared by him of the tape — have a literally hair-raising effect on the audience. ... Both are in agony, the causes of the agony are the same, but it is not the same agony.

Fletcher and Spurling, *Beckett,* p. 92

It is a new tone and a new direction for Beckett's writing. All his earlier work is about depression in its various manifestations, from mere boredom to near catatonia, with appropriate attendant symptoms. In comparison, *Krapp's Last Tape* is far more human open, and available. Its subject is not depression, but grief, and instead of shying away from its causes, it shows, poignantly and with great beauty, precisely what has been lost.

A. Alvarez, *Beckett,* p. 99

Rough for Theatre I
and Rough for Theatre II

Theatrical sketches.
Written: in French, in the 1950s.
Published: in *Ends and Odds* (New York: Grove Press, 1976).
   Theatre I first published as *Fragment de theatre* in *Minuit* 8
   (Mar. 1974).

Like W.B. Yeats's late play, The Cat and the Moon, *Theatre I features A, a blind man, and B, a cripple. They meet by chance, and B hatches the idea that they might form a symbiotic partnership: he could serve as the eyes, and A as the legs, and between*

them they could form a whole being with a better chance of sur-
vival. Each once had a woman; now they have no one to help
them. B is the pragmatist, while A keeps asking questions – about
the light, the trees, their immediate surroundings. B is reticent,
never seems to have noticed these things: 'A: Will it not soon be
light? B: Day ... night ... It seems to me sometimes the earth
must have got stuck, one sunless day, in the heart of winter, in
the grey of evening.' B becomes irritable, even strikes A, but like
Hamm in Endgame, *also in a wheelchair, he needs A. At B's*
request, A tucks the blanket around B's one remaining leg, but
then remains kneeling, and B becomes more annoyed. The sketch
ends in uneasiness, and simmering violence.

In Theatre II, *two men, A and B, arrive to assess the life of C, who*
stands motionless, back to the audience, ready to jump out the
apartment window. Their task, presumably, is to decide his fate
based on the documents they have brought with them – primarily
quotations from C's acquaintances. Although the development is
weak, some of the testimony is hilarious. A and B consider the
bits and scraps of C's life, including his confessed 'morbid sensi-
tivity to the opinion of others'. They seem, however, just as
interested in the erratic electric light and the love-birds they
find in a cage as they are in C's predicament. They finally decide
to 'let him jump', only to discover that he is already dead.

Embers

Radio play in one act.
First London production: BBC Third Programme, 24 June 1959
  (dir. Donald McWhinnie; with Jack McGowran).
Stage production: French Graduate Circle of Edinburgh, Edinburgh Festival, 1977.
Published: in *Evergreen Review,* Nov-Dec. 1959; London: Faber
  and Faber; New York: Grove Press, 1960.

Embers *is set on the ocean's edge, with the continuous sound of*
the sea as background. Henry, alone, speaks to his dead father,
drowned in the sea. He recalls a tale of two old men, Bolton and
Holloway, standing before the fire on a freezing night ('not a
sound, only the fire, no flames now, embers. (Pause) *Embers').*

Bolton is in great need and distress, but the story is never finished. Henry's wife, Ada, converses with him, but because her voice is 'low and remote throughout', and because no sound accompanies her movements, we do not know whether she is present in fact or only in Henry's mind. The couple, too, recall images, but fail in recreating them. Like the fire, the conversation is reduced to embers, and Ada warns of the time 'there will be no other voice in the world but yours'. So the play ends with Henry talking to himself once again, recalling the dying man in pain, and finally, 'Ah yes, the waste. (Pause) Words. (Pause) Saturday . . . nothing, Sunday . . . Sunday . . . nothing all day. . . . Not a sound'.

In the BBC production of 1957, *All That Fall* came across on the whole splendidly. *Embers,* two years later, was less happy, Henry's voice, aged and cracked, being of so stylized a decrepitude that it was difficult in the extreme to make out the words, the all-important words. . . . The reason *Embers* failed entails a problem that has beset Beckett's work since *Endgame.* He has been preoccupied since then with illusion . . . preoccupied with solipsism, with lonely people haunted by interior voices, with peoplings that may be the illusions of solitude. And the convention for this illusory place of reality tends to be something that interferes with intelligibility, in performance if not in the script. . . . Such matters call for a delicacy of producer's judgment that has not always been exercised, and also represent on some occasions downright miscalculation on the author's part. For he has pared each work down to a set of minimal clues, which given the additional impediments to reception are likely to leave the audience more irritated than moved.
Hugh Kenner, *Reader's Guide,* p. 163

With *Embers,* as Beckett conceived it, the listener is required to submit his imagination to the command of Henry. . . . The play becomes through this submission an adventure into the labyrinth of consciousness, an exploring with Henry of the many planes of reality: memories, obsessions, unspecifed but urgent fears, wish-fulfilling fantasies, moods, sudden waves of guilt at self-betrayals or moral evasions. . . . Always there is the insistent perception of life in time represented by the rhythm of the sea.
Richard Cave, *Journal of Beckett Studies,* No. 3
(Summer 1978), p. 121

Embers opens with Henry trying to be with his father. . . . As their names suggest, Ada and Addie may not be wife and daughter at all, not even imagined wife and daughter, only father-surrogates: Ada is a near Anagram of Dad and Addie a rhyme for Daddie.

Paul Lawley, *'Embers:* an Interpretation',
Journal of Beckett Studies, No. 6 (Autumn 1980), p. 35

Act without Words II

Mime for two players.
Written: in French, as *Acte sans paroles II*, 1956.
First production: Clarendon Press Institute, Oxford, as part of
    the first Live New Departures Arts Circus, Autumn 1959 (dir.
    John McGrath).
First London production: Institute of Contemporary Arts,
    25 Jan. 1960.
Revived: In-Stage, London 15 July 1962.
Published: Paris: Éditions de minuit, 1957; New York: Grove
    Press, 1960.

*This brief mime shows two players, A and B, in two large sacks
on the stage. The point of a goad prods sack A into movement
and a 'slow, awkward, absent' emergence, to set about his routine
of eating, dressing, and carrying the sacks to a different part of
the stage. He is consistently dishevelled and brooding. Finally he
undresses and re-enters his sack, at which point the goad, supported
this time by a wheel, prods character B into action. 'Brisk, rapid,
and precise', B goes through a more elaborate and precise routine,
constantly checking his watch, and then re-locates the sacks on
the stage and retires into his sack. The mime ends as it began,
with the goad (now on two wheels) awakening character A. The
audience assumes an endless cycle of such activity.*

The two *Acts Without Words* seem to be loosely based on punish-
ments from the classical underworld . . . the second that of
Sisyphus who had to trudge up a hill pushing a boulder which fell
to the bottom every time he reached the top. . . . The mime's two
characters, one sluggish, the other brisk, suggest, as Vladimir and
Estragon sometimes do, two aspects of a single person.

Fletcher and Spurling, *Beckett,* p. 120

When the goad again prods A into prayer, we have come full circle. The sum total of human endeavour is on the surface of the mime play. ... Activities will remain the same for each actor. Life in time accomplishes nothing, however one responds to time, but movements through time can be delectable play.

Ruby Cohn, *Back to Beckett,* p. 177

Rough for Radio I

Sketch for a radio play.
Written: in French, 1961. *Unproduced.*
Published: as 'Sketch for Radio Play', in *Stereo Headphones,*
    No. 7 (Spring 1976); and in *Ends and Odds.*

A precursor to Cascando *and* Words and Music, *this sketch offers another attempt to bring words and music under control. The main character, designated only as 'He', is briefly joined by 'She', who has come to listen to Voice and Music, 'He's' incessant companions. A knob switches on first Voice, then Music, but they are very faint; they 'are not together', can neither see nor hear each other. 'She' leaves, whereupon 'He' places an urgent phone call to a doctor concerning the plight of Voice and Music: 'they're ending ... ENDING' and 'they're together ... TOGETHER ... like ... one ... the breathing'. 'He' is left with a promise of 'confinement' by noon of the following day, though we never know whether the confinement applies to him or his companions. But both Voice and Music are feeble and fading fast. Beckett has no intention that this play should be produced because it has been overtaken by* Cascando.

Rough for Radio II

Radio play.
Written: in French, early 1960s.
First broadcast: BBC Radio 3, 13 Apr. 1976 (dir. Martin Esslin;
    with Harold Pinter, Billie Whitelaw, and Patrick Magee).
Published: as *Pochade Radiophonique,* in *Minuit,* 16 (Nov. 1975);
    and in *Ends and Odds.*

The voices heard in this drama are those of Animator, Stenographer, and Fox. There is also a silent character named Dick, whose job is, at the Animator's bidding, to beat Fox with a ruler until he produces dialogue, which the Stenographer records verbatim. Each time Fox pauses, the other two try to interpret what he has just uttered, and then Fox is hit again. When Fox finally names someone from his past in his narrative, Animator is finally convinced that they are getting somewhere. He orders Stenographer to kiss Fox, whereupon the victim faints, and the inquisitors are left musing over and (more insidiously) altering slightly what they have heard. The short piece is both sinister and funny in tone. One cannot help thinking of Fox as a writer, forced into 'inspiration' and subject to the whims of readers and critics. But this inquisition also resembles a Nazi interrogation, since the questioners, too, are prisoners of some mysterious superiors who write reports on the results of these questionings: 'We ... note yet again with pain that these dicta ... like all those communicated to date and by reason of the same deficiencies, are totally inacceptable'.

The interest of the play resides in its involvement with traditional considerations of radio drama such as indication of character through voice and tone. In the BBC production the voice of Animator is educated and authoritative to the point of arrogance, but is subject to lapses into a romantic tone. The stenographer sounds absurdly pert and well organized and only occasionally loses the cool composure of an efficient personal secretary. Patrick Magee's Fox is a voice one associates with *the* persona of Beckett's radio drama, a remote voice which is wavering and inconsequential, otherworldy in its relationship to the voices which surround it and command it to speak.

Fletcher, et. al., Student's Guide, p. 166

Happy Days

Play in two acts.
Written: in English, 1960; *translated* into French as *Oh les beaux jours* by Beckett.
First American production: Cherry Lane Th., New York, 17 Sept. 1961 (dir. Alan Schneider).

First London production: Royal Court Th., 1 Nov. 1962 (dir.
George Devine).
First Paris production: Odéon Théâtre de France, 15 Nov. 1963
(dir. Roger Blin, supervised by Beckett).
Revived: in French, Teatro del Ricotto, Venice, at the Internation-
al Festival of Prose Drama, 28 Sept. 1963; National Th., at the
Old Vic, London,13 Mar. 1975 (dir. Peter Hall); Royal Court
Th., London, 7 June 1979 (dir. Beckett); Public Th., New
York, Oct. 1979 (dir. Andrei Serban); BBC TV, Oct. 1979;
BBC 2, 12 Nov. 1982 (dir. Beckett).
Published: New York: Grove Press, 1961; London: Faber and
Faber, 1962; Paris: Éditions de minuit, 1963.

Happy Days *presents us with Winnie, an incurable optimist of
about fifty, 'embedded up to her waist in exact centre of mound'.
Winnie's husband, Willie, appears only occasionally from his
tunnel behind the mound, but that does not impede Winnie from
talking to him while he reads the newspaper and is only sparingly
provoked to reply. Winnie's opening observation, 'Another heaven-
ly day', sets the tone for the entire monologue, and it is carried
on even in Act II, when Winnie is buried up to her neck in the
mound and can no longer busy herself with the contents of a
capacious handbag which is her comfort and diversion in Act I.
Winnie faithfully follows the routine of her day – praying, brush-
ing her teeth, reminiscing about the past ('the old style'), endlessly
trying to recall 'unforgettable lines' which she has once read.
Like Hamm in* Endgame, *she is trying to kill time, but she doesn't
have a straight man – Willie rarely replies. Unlike Hamm, she
seems oblivious to the encroaching end, and is willing to proclaim
the vacuum of her life* 'another *happy day'.*

Happy Days is, of course, Samuel Beckett's latest dramatic comment on the irony, pathos, and chronic hopelessness of the human
condition. . . . It strikes me . . . as the least of his dramatic efforts.
The language, enjoying none of that poetic intensity which so
embodied *Krapp* and *Godot,* is flat and prosaic; the symbols are
almost nude in their unambiguousness; and those repetitions of
which Beckett is so fond . . . have finally become rather boring.
. . . *Happy Days* is too predictable; so obvious, in fact, that I
experienced the uncomfortable sensation, before the evening was

five minutes old, that I had written the play myself and was none
too pleased with my handiwork.

Robert Brustein, New Republic, 2 Oct. 1961, p. 45-6,
reprinted in Seasons of Discontent, p. 53-6

The first thing we are happy to say about *Happy Days* is that
Mr. Beckett has consented at last to allow woman her fair share
of human futility. . . . We had long since taken for granted that in
Mr. Beckett's view life's intolerable tedium and pointlessness were
noticed only by men and that they alone suffered the grief of
being alive and the chagrin of being unable to die. . . . *Happy
Days* has corrected this imbalance. . . . For there is surely no
longer any doubt that women suffer in a special way. Women are
not men. It is unkind and illegal to assume that they are. If women
were men, marriage would not be the same problem at all. Marriage
is a life-long union between two opposing sorts of pain. . . . What
a mercy for the unfortunate man that his wife is buried up to
the waist in scorched earth! She cannot take steps to *make* him
hear, which she would certainly do if Mr. Beckett had not had the
wisdom to bury her. Wisdom? Well, not wisdom, perhaps. Just a
small prejudice in favour of his own sex. An appreciation of how
much deafness matters to a married man. The lengths to which he
will go to ensure it.

Nigel Dennis, Encounter, Jan. 1963, p. 37

Winnie is frightfully busy doing nothing, the way I feel I am a lot
of the time. The play's about getting on with it, getting through
the day, and trying not to be too depressed. And it's about needing someone else, if only to shout at. How many marriages do we
know like that? And how many people?

Billie Whitelaw, who played Winnie, interviewed by
Benedict Nightingale in Radio Times, 13-19 Oct. 1979, p. 21

The first sound is the prompter's bell, and almost her first words
– 'Begin, Winnie' – are like the words of an actress steeling herself to play the part one more time. . . . Tomorrow, she reflects,
there will be another parasol to put up (though it, too, will burn),
and tomorrow the little mirror she breaks on a stone . . . will be
intact again in her bag, if the property-master is not negligent.
. . . Beckett has invoked the repeatability of the play before, the
plight of actors trapped in parts, but never so deftly, never with

such buoyant pathos. . . . All the world's a stage, all the world's a Woolworth's; there are always more parasols, more looking-glasses, more words.

Hugh Kenner, *Reader's Guide,* p. 149

Words and Music

Radio play.
Written: in English, 1961.
First production: BBC Third Programme, 13 Nov. 1962.
Published: in *Evergreen Review,* Nov.-Dec. 1962.

In Words and Music . . . *the process [of creation] is acted out by three characters: Croak, a poet, and his two servants, Words and Music, whom he calls Joe and Bob. At the beginning Music, a small orchestra, is tuning up while Words proses on repetitively, abstractly, polysyllabically, and unpunctuated about that old favourite of Beckett's, sloth. Croak shuffles in and brings them to order with a club. The theme tonight, he announces, is Love. Words immediately repeats his same dull prosing, substituting Love for Sloth. Croak is anguished. He summons Music to try for something more appropriate, but with no greater success. Croak tries cajoling them and Words responds with some grandiose rhetoric. . . . Croak suggests another theme, Age, and becomes more agonized and more violent in his rejection of his two servants' paltry attempts. Very gradually, protestingly, Words and Music clear their throats of hesitations, platitudes, and periphrases. A poem tentatively emerges, phrase by phrase, Words and Music helping each other on until both are softly singing together. Finally, the first two themes, Love and Age, are brought success-fully into unison: an old man with his old love to tend him. The next stage is the particular: 'The face', Croak commands. . . . In the end, the poem is finished, subtle, touching, precise, and, incidentally, better than almost any of the poems Beckett has published on their own. Croak abruptly drops his club and shuffles away, leaving Words pleading with Music to repeat his part of the work that has cost them both so much.*

It is a brilliant, witty, utterly original dramatization of the labour and frustrations of creation, the poet alternatively bullying and despairing, his instruments inept, unwieldly, and only slowly, despite themselves, becoming usable; then the final letdown when there is nothing more to be done. It also illustrates vividly that split between the music the poet hears in his head and the leaden words at his command, and the slow, unwilling process of disciplining and refining those two elements until they finally chime together in a single work of art.

A. Alvarez, *Beckett,* p. 119-20

Words and Music in particular resembles an intricate rich Symbolist poem composed in a medium still more suggestive than Mallarmé's printed language, a medium of pure audition. It is the most profound, the most original use to which Beckett has put radio, and one is tempted to say as original and moving a use as any to which radio has been put. I regret that I have only an intuitive base for this judgment. I have no idea how the music is meant to sound — John Beckett's score for *Words and Music* is unpublished. ...

Hugh Kenner, *Reader's Guide,* p. 169

Beckett's preoccupation with the process of human consciousness as an incessant verbal flow . . . here found its logical culmination, and one which only radio could provide. For, after all, human consciousness . . . does not only consist of a constant stream of language. It has a non-verbal component as well, the parallel and no less unbroken stream of wordless consciousness of being made up of body-sensations, inner tensions, the awareness of body temperature, aches, pains, the throbbings of the flow of one's own blood. . . . This stream of non-verbal life-awareness, of life-force or *Will,* is the subject matter of *music* which portrays and represents the ebb and flow of the emotions. To give an adequate representation of the Beckettian exploration of the self's experience of itself, music therefore had to be added to the verbal stream of consciousness. . . .

Martin Esslin, *Enounter,* Sept. 1975, p. 43

Play

Play in one act.
Written: in English, 1962-63; *translated* into French as *Comédie*

by Beckett.

First production: in German, Ulmer Th., Ulm-Donau, 14 June 1963.

First American production: Cherry Lane Th., New York, 4 Jan. 1964 (dir. Alan Schneider).

First London production: National Th., Old Vic., 7 Apr. 1964 (dir. George Devine; with Billie Whitelaw).

First Paris production: Pavillon de Marson, 14 June 1964 (dir. Jean-Marie Serreau, supervised by Beckett).

Revived: Royal Court Th., May 1976 (dir. Donald McWhinnie); Schiller Th., 6 Oct. 1978 (dir. Beckett).

Film version: as *Comédie,* Serreau, 1966 (dir. Marin Karmitz).

Published: in German, as *Spiel,* in *Theater Heute,* July 1963; Paris: Éditions de minuit; London: Faber and Faber, 1964; and in *Evergreen Review,* New York, 1965.

Three characters, a man (M) and two women (W1 and W2), face the audience from their immobile positions in three separate urns. Each speaks in turn as a bright spotlight cues their remarks, and though they do not speak to or hear each other, their separate stories blend into one story − of the man's adulterous relationship with the two women. Presumably married to W1, he was discovered in his affair with W2. Confronted by W1, he swore that he could not live without her and would end the affair − but could not. In the end each voice, alone, wonders if the other two are together, and both humour and pathos prevail. M wonders if the women 'Meet and sit, now in the one dear old place, now in the other, and sorrow together, and compare − (hiccup) pardon − happy memories'. The piercing, demanding spotlight still searches each character relentlessly for some 'truth' before the final blackout. Then, the entire play is repeated without variation.

Immobilized in three gigantic urns, above which only their tilted heads are visible ... unconscious of each other's presence ... they seem to be imprisoned in one of the lower circles of hell, damned to ruminate eternally on their petty lives and vices. ... Guided by some malicious unseen will, this diabolicial beam sets the rhythm and tone of their damnation. ... Mr. Beckett takes about twelve minutes to complete this eerie tableau, thus proving what a deft poet he is; and he is deftly served by Alan Schneider's precise direction.

Robert Brustein, *New Republic,* 1 Feb. 1964, p. 30

Beckett in Paris at the beginning of the war was a neutral Irishman with arms folded. But Nazi harrassment of his Jewish friends, and Nazi shooting of hostages, conquered his detachment and led to anger, then to action. By the first winter of the Occupation he was collating, editing, and typing scraps of information about troop movements for a far-flung Resistance group that survived nearly two years before a captured man betrayed it under torture. ... Others, who fell into the Gestapo's hands, would have been in the position of many of his protagonists, repeatedly commanded to talk without knowing what it was they were expected to say. ... It was only after twenty years, in 1963, that he used the stark situation directly, in the play called (grimly) *Play* in which a man and two women rehearse and rehearse their unsatisfactory testimony at the whim of an inquisitorial spotlight. This is perhaps a glimpse, tentative and to be used with caution, into the psychology of his creative process: a sense of having been solicited by realities so nearly unbearable that art can only come to terms with them slowly, through substitutions, at many tentative removes, until when the actuality is approximated it has been so purified of circumstance we do not recognize it for what it is. The central metaphor of *Play*, the immobilized speakers accosted by the light, has drawn down contempt for its formulaic despairingness, or its alleged want of meaning, from a generation of journalists who know perfectly well about the SS.

Hugh Kenner, *Reader's Guide*, p. 72-3

I think that *Play* is a quartet; not a trio at all. The light is a very positive part, a very frightening part. ... It was an instrument of torture. ... I remember that my doctor came to see what we were doing, when I told him I wasn't sleeping very well, and he said that if you did that night after night, you would go completely out of your mind.

Billie Whitelaw, interview with James Knowlson, 1 Feb. 1977, *Journal of Beckett Studies*, No. 3 (Summer 1978), p. 86

The text fell into three parts: *Chorus* (all characters speaking simultaneously); *Narration* (in which the characters talk about the events which led to the catastrophe); and *Meditation* (in which they reflect on their state of being endlessly suspended in limbo). These three parts are repeated, and the play ends, as it began, with the Chorus.

Beckett, quoted by Martin Esslin, *Encounter*, Sept. 1975, p. 44

It occurred to [Beckett] in Paris, while watching the first run-throughs of *Comédie*, that the second reading of the script might work just as well if it were not a strict repetition of the first act. He likened it to 'the light growing tired' and wrote to Devine to describe it: 'According to the text it is rigorously identical with the first statement. We now think it would be dramatically more effective to have it express a slight weakening, both of question and of response, by means of less and perhaps slower light and correspondingly less volume and speed of voice. . . . The whole idea involves a spot mechanism of greater flexibility than has seemed necessary so far. The inquirer (light) beginning to emerge as no less a victim of his inquiry than they and as needing to be free, within narrow limits, literally to act the part, i.e., to vary if only slightly his speeds and intensities.'

Cascando

Radio play, with score by Marcel Mihalovici.
Written: in French, 1962.
First broadcast: in French, ORTF, 13 Oct. 1963 (dir. Roger Blin).
First English broadcast: BBC Third Programme, 6 Oct. 1964
    (dir. Donald McWhinnie).
Published: in *Dramatische Dichtungen,* I (1963); and in *Evergreen Review,* May-June 1963.

In Cascando, *Opener commands both Voice and Music. Opener tells us that people used to say these were in his head. He no longer protests, since others neither see nor understand him; but he insists that Voice and Music bear 'no resemblance' to him. He merely 'opens' their performance. Voice tells – or, more accurately, fails to tell – of Woburn, a huge man who is running through sand, up and down slopes, falling, getting up, urging himself to continue despite his exhaustion. But neither Woburn nor the Voice ever finish, although Voice constantly admonishes himself to* get it right *this time. Intermittently, Opener stills Voice and 'opens' Music, and, as the play progresses, calls on Voice and Music together, encouraging them to act in harmony. Voice winds down – cannot finish, but cannot stop; like the artist, he is condemned to recreate the story.*

Beckett, quoted by Dierdre Bair, *Samuel Beckett,* p. 478

'Cascando' is itself a musical term, describing the dying away of sound – slowing down of tempo, diminishing of volume. ... *Cascando* is Beckett's only play since *Fin de partie* to be written in French, and it absorbs the narrative problems with which he wrestled in the French fiction: how tell a story; and why? Or, conversely, how be silent as long as the mind churns words? *Cascando,* buried as it is in the creative imagination, seems irrelevant to any world at large. As in the case of Beckett's French fiction, however, the imagination has had to live *through* the world in order to retire into what it hopes to find as itself. There has to be a melody before cascando.

Ruby Cohn, *Back to Beckett,* p. 202-4

The flavour, the whole quality that makes his despair unbearable and even lively lies in the words, that inimitable partnership of misery, music hall, and English prose tradition.

John Holmstrom, *New Statesman,* 16 Oct. 1964, quoted in
Fletcher and Spurling, *Beckett,* p. 147

Voice is the eternal Beckett narrator, whipping himself on to tell just one more story in the vain hope that it will be the unattainable right one that, when finished, will allow him to rest in silence. ... *Cascando* is in itself an 'expressive act', a dramatization of the artist's 'fidelity to failure'. So Opener, driven on by the hope of resting after a last 'right' story, is faithful not to his inner voices but simply to his function: 'I open and close'. *Cascando* is less witty and dramatic than *Words and Music* and pursues a less satisfying quarry: not a finished poem, but a story that is, as it has to be, broken and unending. Even so, it dramatizes once again a complex, agonized aesthetic in a peculiarly direct way.

A. Alvarez, *Beckett,* p. 120-2

Film

Screenplay.
Written: in English, 1963.
Filmed: in New York, Summer 1964 (dir. Alan Schneider,
    supervised by Beckett; with Buster Keaton).
First shown: New York Film Festival, 1965. Remade by British
    Film Institute, 1979 (dir. David Clark, with Max Wall).
Published: London: Faber and Faber, 1967.

Film, Beckett notes, is divided into three parts: the street (eight minutes), the stairs (five minutes), and the room (seventeen minutes). The foundation for the film is from Berkeley's philosophy: *esse est percipi* ('To be is to be perceived'). which implies that the universe is dependent for its existence on God's continual perception of it. The two central 'characters' are O, the Object or protagonist and E, the Eye or pursuing camera.

In the first shot human beings move in couples down a street, all in the same direction . . . Except O. In long coat and hat on this summer day, he hugs a wall as he makes his furtive way against the general direction of movement. In blind haste, he jostles an elderly couple, who stop to look at him, she raising her lorgnon, *he his* pince-nez. *They look after O, but they are looked at by E, so that they experience 'an agony of perceivedness'. O enters a dark doorway. Hiding from footsteps, O is not perceived by a little old flower-woman, who also experiences 'an agony of perceivedness' when E has her in sight. O hastens upstairs to unlock a door into a 'small barely furnished room,' in which are a large cat and a small dog, a parrot in a cage and a goldfish in a bowl. All the animals have eyes. The room's single window and mirror present a threat of eyes, and O hastens to cover them, as in a house of mourning. With meticulous patience, he eventually manages to eject both dog and cat, he tears a print of God in four, and he covers the cage and bowl, escaping from assorted eyes. Seated in a rocking chair, he inspects seven ages of his life, committed to photographs. In all but the last someone's eyes inspect his face – his mother in the first two, then a dog, the college rector, his fiancee, a little girl. In the last picture O is thirty, looking over forty; hat and overcoat designate him as the man we have been sleuthing. . . . Moving backward through his seven ages, O tears each of his photographs in four. . . . When O dozes off, semi-secure in his rocking chair, the camera finally catches him full-face, but with head bowed. . . . The latter starts up, opening his eye; the other eye is covered by a patch. We cut to E, a blurred image but clearly the same face – one eye and one patch, a nail at the temple above the patch, and on the face an expression of 'acute* intentness'. *We cut back to O, who closes his eye, covers his face with his hands, begins to rock in his chair. After a cut back to E 'as before', we cut again to O, who bows his*

head, face buried in his hands, till the rocking dies down and the
movie ends. The perceiving eye has trapped its object.

Ruby Cohn, *Back to Beckett,* p. 206

In an unusual remark to a reporter, Beckett himself summarized
Film: It's a movie about the perceiving eye, about the perceived
and the perceiver — two aspects of the same man. The perceiver
desires like mad to perceive, and the perceived tries deperately to
hide. Then, in the end, one wins.

Ruby Cohn, *Back to Beckett,* p. 207

We are entitled to draw a final conclusion, that if the camera
stands for ourselves, and resembles him, then he too is ourselves,
evading that gaze, We, too, in entering the darkened place where
we watch films, all of us facing the same direction, have sought
refuge from all eyes including our own; and we, too, when the
perceiving face looks intently out toward us from the screen,
encounter in amazement ourselves. In the film as it was produced
in 1964 all this is shaky. Beckett's script professes frank uncertainty
about cinematic devices, Alan Schneider had never directed a film
before nor Grove Press produced one, there was too little time
available in the interlocking schedules of indispensable people.
... Mainly, the crucial distinction between the two kinds of
images — the protagonist's perception of the room the camera's
perception of him perceiving — was insufficiently emphatic to be
recognized at once as a convention. ... A philosophical film
which is in part about the order of escape we are indulging in
when we go film-watching remains a conception of potential
interest, and one wishes that, like a play whose first production
has been unsatisfactory, it could be realized anew. But there was
only one Keaton.

Hugh Kenner, *Reader's Guide,* p. 169

Though Beckett may stand here in opposition to the avant-garde
cinema whose main tendency is, in fact, to achieve a confusion of
the multiple elements of the film, his attempt, as with his theatre
and fiction, is to return to the essence of the medium. This in
itself represents an avant-garde effort. . . . Though eagerly awaited
by Beckett's admirers, *Film* received a rather cold and negative
reception at the Third New York Film Festival both from audience
and reviewers. In general, it was found 'vacuous and pretentious,

too simple, too obvious in its symbolism. ... We the quasi-sophisticated theatregoing audience, the faithfuls of art films too often expect from writers such as Beckett messages of deep philosophical means. ... We are no longer satisfied with the obvious, and yet what seemed so 'obvious' in this film is, in fact, its main theme: the simple reaffirmation of the essence of cinema, that is to say, visual expression of life and movement through photographic manipulation.... It is, therefore, logical that Beckett's first film should use as its subject its own essence: visual perception. In other words, if Beckett's concern in the novel is to expose the agony of linguistic expression, and in the theatre to reveal the agony of verbal and gestic expression, then, turning to motion pictures, the message he wants to impart is what he himself defines in the screenplay as the 'agony of perceivedness'. ... Visual perception alone (as exemplified in *Film*) results in frustration and failure. This is indeed a paradoxical process of creation, but a process to which Beckett has remained stubbornly faithful in his effort to create works of art which contain their own critical and analytical judgment. As one of Beckett's own creator-heroes proclaims: to make of failure 'a howling success'.

Raymond Federman, *Film Quarterly,* Winter 1966-67, p. 46-51, quoted in *Critical Heritage,* p. 275-83.

Come and Go

'Dramaticule' in one act.
Written: in English, 1965; *translated* into French as *Va et vient* by Beckett.
First production: in German, as *Kommen und Gehen,* Schiller Th., Berlin, 14 Jan. 1966.
First English-language production: Peacock Th., Dublin, 28 Feb, 1968.
First London production: Royal Festival Hall, 9 Dec. 1968.
First New York production: by Mabou Mines, Th. for the New City, 23 Oct. 1975 (dir. Lee Breur).
Published: Paris: Éditions de minuit, 1966; London: Calder and Boyars, 1967.

This very brief play shows three women, Vi, Ru, and Flo, sitting on a bench and facing the audience, reminiscing about old school days. Each character leaves the stage briefly, and in her absence the other two exchange an appalling secret about the missing third. This information (perhaps about a terminal illness?), whispered by one character in the other's ear, is never revealed to the audience. We know only that all three have changed in some disturbing way, and that each is unaware of the change in herself. The news produces the same response – an appalled 'Oh' – each time. The three finally clasp hands and the play closes with the cryptic comment, 'I can feel the rings', even though Beckett specifies that no rings should be apparent. The figures are obscured with full-length coats and hats that shade their faces, the bench is not visible ('It should not be clear what they are sitting on'), and 'they should disappear a few steps from the lit area'.

Vi, Flo and Ru, three characters again; but unlike the three people in *Play*, who were at each other's throats, the three women in *Come and Go* (with an unstated epigraph by Eliot: In the room the women come and go/Talking of Michelangelo), are delicately solicitous of one another's susceptibilities, and do not chatter of Michelangelo at all but define themselves by what they do not say. Each is (we gather) doomed. . . . It is a beautiful, delicate, decorous work; if the scale of the action falls below the 'certain magnitude' Aristotle specified, well, so much the worse; and if there is no way to make it the culmination of a theatrical evening, it is a pity we demand so much of a theatre evening. . . . It is a play made of what they do not say; of silence, of silences.

Hugh Kenner, *Reader's Guide,* p. 174

The three women of *Come and Go* are dressed in turn-of-the-century coats and hats, which recall Chekhov's *Three Sisters.* The first full line of dialogue – Vi's 'When did we three last meet?' – echoes the three witches of *Macbeth.* A few lines later . . . they are three little maids from school. . . . During their few minutes on stage, we may wonder whether they are the three fates. Ringed with these shadowy suggestions, the three women are faintly illuminated by their monosyllabic names – Vi, Ru, Flo. They *vie* for arcane information; they express *rue* – 'oh!', life *flows* on. . . . As the three women have come from and gone into stage darkness, they have come from and will go into eternal darkness. . . . They will never go to Moscow, they will never be consulted by a hero, they will never outgrow their schooldays, and each pair of them will not quite scissor the other's life. Like us all, they 'come and go' on earth — briefly.

Ruby Cohn, *Back to Beckett*, p. 211—12

Eh Joe

Television play in one act.
Written: in English, 1965.
First production: In German, Suddeutscher Rundfunk Stuttgart,
 13 Apr. 1966 (dir. Beckett).
First English production: BBC Television, 4 July 1966 (dir.
 Beckett and Alan Gibson; with Jack McGowran).
Published: London: Faber and Faber, 1967

*This relentlessly bleak play consists of a woman's voice speaking
to a lone figure, Joe. We see him first checking his shabby room
to ensure that he is alone; then he sits on his bed, listening intently to the disembodied voice as the camera slowly moves in to
a close-up of his face. Obviously a haunting voice from his past,
the woman taunts him with his past callousness: 'The best's yet
to come, you said that last time. . . . Hurrying me into my coat.
. . . Last time I was favoured with from you. . . . Say it now, Joe,
no one will hear you. . . . Come on, Joe, no one can say it like
you, say it again now and listen to yourself. . . . The best's to
come.' No one loves him now, and the voice from 'that penny-
farthing hell you call your mind' reminds him of another young
woman whom he used and abandoned, and who killed herself out
of loneliness, first trying to drown, then to use a razor, and finally
taking sleeping pills before lying down on the rocks at the ocean
shore:* 'There's love for you. . . . *Isn't it, Joe? . . . Wasn't it, Joe?
. . . Eh Joe?' Both voice and image fade. Waiting for the cessation
of his voices and for his own death, Joe is like one in his own
circle of hell.*

Joe is Mr. Beckett's man in the only situation Mr. Beckett has
bothered to consider since *Waiting for Godot;* everything is over
and nothing has been worth the effort it has cost. Joe has, we
gather, been a successful lecher and the Voice tells the story of
how a girl he once loved had, after two unsuccessful attempts,
killed herself in a particular place by the sea. Joe says nothing;

43

he sits, and his expression alone indicates that he remembers everything he is told. In this narrow, intense world where everything is compressed to the point of crisis which contains both explanation and consequence, Mr. Beckett is a master. The Voice (Miss Sian Phillips) was given a monologue in which rhythms, images, and epithets often caught and illuminated the mind. *Eh Joe* began in silence, with titles undecorated in delightfully simple typography. While the Voice spoke, the camera held Mr. Jack MacGowran in close-up. Lighting and photography helped but Mr. MacGowran, intense, ravaged by pride and regret, soundlessly trying at the end of memory to say something which might have been an attempt at self-justification, offered a performance not quickly to be forgotten.

The Times, 5 July 1966, p. 5

This work invites comparison with *Play*, but what it lacks is *Play's* complex ironies. This is not to say that it isn't a competent piece of television writing (it is, by any fair standard of what constitutes the norm of dramatic composition for the medium), but simply that it is little more. Judged by Beckett's own standards it's a slender playlet, making one point well enough but going no further. The decision to select, as the prosecution in the case of another and less fortunate woman, one of Joe's happily resettled cast-offs, leads Beckett into a rare lapse of taste. . . . Not only is this an error of tact, it's a tactical error, since the watcher would normally expect this speaker to be the centre of the ensuing action. By the time he has recovered his bearings, the point is lost. . . . Perhaps the relative weakness of *Eh Joe* is simply that it is *too* simple.

Spurling and Fletcher, *Beckett,* p. 99

Eh Joe is Beckett's most intimate and precise image of the anguish he has devoted most of his creative life to describing: a man shut off on his own in a sealed room, tortured by an unforgiving multitude of voices. This is like the world of the schizophrenic which Murphy, in his innocence, admired and yearned for. But now it is presented in its full horror, from the inside. . . . In terms of the medium, it is also wholly original. In a sense, it had to be, for there was no way in which Beckett could otherwise have accommodated the alien form of television to his overriding obsession with the inner world. The essential characteristic of both film and television is that everything should be subordinate to the eye; the audience is made to see not only with their eyes, but also with their ears and minds, absorbed into a compelling alternate reality which, at its best, is as immediate and engulfing as a dream. . . . Beckett's solution was to stand the usual procedure on its head, making the language itself take over the function of the camera. . . . Instead of varying the visual images, Beckett makes the language itself continually cut from one detail to another in a kind of verbal montage.

Not I

Play in one act.

Written: in English, 1972; *translated* into French as *Pas moi* by Beckett.

First American production: Lincoln Center, New York, as part of a Beckett Festival, 22 Nov. 1972 (dir. Alan Schneider; with Jessica Tandy).

First London production: Royal Court Th., 16 Jan. 1973 (dir. Anthony Page; with Billie Whitelaw).

First Paris production: Théâtre d'Orsay, 1976 (dir. Serreau; with Madeleine Renaud).

Revived: Théâtre d'Orsay, Paris, 11 Apr. 1978 (dir. Beckett).

Published: London: Faber and Faber, 1973; New York: Grove Press, 1974; Paris: Éditions de minuit, 1975.

Not I *is a monologue spoken by a Mouth to a silent Auditor. Already speaking when the curtain opens, Mouth continues in broken phrases for the duration of the fifteen-minute play, telling of a 'she', never acknowledging that they are Mouth's own experiences. With 'vehement refusal to relinquish the third person', Mouth speaks of a child, born prematurely, abandoned by her parents, loveless – now seventy years old. Suddenly this old woman, while silently wandering in a field, is overcome with darkness. Thinking at first that this may be punishment for unnamed sins, she finds herself speaking, her words tumbling out uncontrollably. We learn that she has hardly spoken a word for years, that she didn't even enter a 'guilty' or 'not guilty' plea at her own trial. Only once or twice a year in winter has she ventured out shopping in silence. Now she pours out her confession*
A. Alvarez, *Beckett,* p. 101-3

45

to the robed Auditor, who merely raises his arms 'in a gesture of silent compassion'.

In Malta [Beckett] had seen Caravaggio's painting of the beheading of St. John and said he was struck by it as 'a voice crying in the wilderness'. ... Then, in Morocco, he was sitting in a sunny cafe one afternoon ... when he saw the second part of the inspiration for *Not I*. An Arab woman shrouded in a *jellaba* was hunkered down on the edge of the sidewalk – in Beckett's words, 'crouched in an attitude of intense waiting'. ... Beckett combined the darkness and drama of the Caravaggio painting with the Arab woman's intensity of waiting and created a mouth, a vivid red gash, the only visible object at the centre of an altogether dark stage. Off to one side he placed a figure described as everything from 'a huge, silent Druidic figure to a grotesquely tall, monk-like figure'.

Dierdre Bair, *Samuel Beckett,* p. 524

All Beckett's dramas play uniqueness against repetition, but *Not I* does so with syntactical daring that is matched only in *Comment c'est.* Incomplete sentences reflect the incomplete stage presence – a mouth – and the story of a still incomplete life. ... The female stage mouth knows as little as the fictional voices about the provenance of words, and it denies knowing what they mean, intermittently refusing to acknowledge that they mean anything. The refrain is familiar in Beckettland, but *we* know that the words have prismatic meanings. So in *Not I.* They create five scenes that summarize human experience: 1) a loveless premature birth, 2) survival through silent list-shopping at the supermarket, 3) the presence of tears in the palm of the hand and the awareness of owning those tears, 4) the silence under court-room questioning, and 5) five times evoked, the April morning when this late spring speech erupted. Economically, Beckett has sketched images for a life whose resonance is extensible to us all – born too soon, surviving mechanically, feeling and watching ourselves feel, wondering about the meaning of the living as we live.

Ruby Cohn, *Back to Beckett,* p. 214-15

The nearest I can come to describing *Not I* is to say that it is an aural mosaic of words, which come pell-mell but not always helter-skelter, and that once it is over, a life, emotions, and a state of mind have been made manifest, with a literally stunning impact upon the audience. Even then, much of the play remains, and should remain, mysterious and shadowy. It opens in total darkness. A woman's voice is heard (but so quietly that it almost mingles with the rattlings of programmes out front), whispering and crying and laughing and then speaking in a brogue, but so quickly that one can barely distinguish the words. Then a spotlight picks out a mouth moving; that is all the lighting there is, from beginning to end. The words never stop coming, and their speed never slackens; they are, we finally realize, the pent-up words of a lifetime, and they are more than the woman can control. . . . This production lasts about fifteen minutes. They are about as densely packed as any fifteen minutes I can remember.

Edith Oliver, *New Yorker,* 2 Dec. 1972, p. 124

All Beckett's plays may be seen as threnodies to wasted lives; but *Not I* is more concrete in its characterization than most, and as starkly visual as any in its evocation of the all-but-invisible piece of human driftwood whose monologue it is. It is also unusually painful – tearing into you like a grappling iron and dragging you after it, with or without your leave. . . . It is a performance of sustained intensity, all sweat, clenched muscle and foaming larynx, and one which finds its variety only upwards: a frantic cackle at the idea that there might be a merciful God; a scream of suffering designed to appease this uncertain deity. But it must be admitted that this breathless pace combines with the incoherence of the character's thoughts to make the piece hard to follow: which is why I'd suggest that it be played twice a session (though this might prove too much even for Miss Whitelaw's athletic throat), or that spectators should first buy and con the script. . . . After all, one of the many assumptions which Beckett's work challenges is that a play should necessarily strip and show its all (or even much of itself) at first encounter. Like good music, *Not I* demands familiarity, and is, I suspect, capable of giving growing satisfaction with each hearing.

Benedict Nightingale, *New Statesman,* 26 Jan. 1973, p. 135-6
quoted in *Critical Heritage,* p. 329-33

That Time

Play in one act.
Written: in English, 1974-75; *translated* into French as *Cette fois* by Beckett.

First London production: Royal Court Th., 20 May 1976 (dir.
Donald McWhinnie).
First American production: Arena Stage, Kreeger Th., Washington,
D.C., Dec. 1976 (dir. Alan Schneider).
Published: London: Faber and Faber, 1976; Paris: Éditions de
minuit, 1978; and in *Ends and Odds*.

The main character in That Time *is again a listener bombarded
with three voices (presumably all his own) recounting his past.
Only his face, surrounded by a shock of white hair, is visible, and
his slow breathing is audible. The three voices, A, B, and C, each
recall separate stories, but they are interspersed and alternated.
'A' tells of the man's return to the scene of his childhood – to
the 'ruin' where the child used to sit among the rocks and imagine
playmates. But having made the ferry trip, he could no longer get
to the old spot, and so had to huddle on a doorstep awaiting the
return ferry, unable to verify the past: 'was it that time . . . or
was that another time all that another time was there ever any
other time but that time away to hell out of it all and never
come back'. 'C' recalls a time when the man, old by then, escaped
from the winter rain into the portrait gallery, where he sat
huddled until evicted, and then slipped into the library, turning
leaves of old books and raising dust. The voice asserts that he was
'never the same after that', could no longer say 'I'. 'B's' memory
is of a woman with whom there were vows of love. He remembers
being with her in a wheat field and on the sand, but finally only
the times that he was alone, trying to hold on to her image, even
making up memories.*

Anyone who expects a new serenity from the seventy-year-old
Beckett should go and be disabused by the birthday celebrations
at the Court. His spiritual migraine is worse than ever. In *Waiting
for Godot* the two main characters had a jaunty resilience about
them. They shared a gallows humour, and even seemed to care for
one another. . . . But now, 21 years later, there is no laughter, no
sharing or caring, and nothing to hope for from the infinite void
beyond. . . . This is the theatre of total introversion – and yet,
surprisingly, the audience is left with a strong objective sense of
the wretched lives on display. . . . All we see in *That Time* is Patrick
Magee's face, eyes mostly shut, hair flaring backwards as if he

were some unearthly blend of Ibsen in his wild old age and the Michelangelo God. But here is another tramp, another tale of disintegration. . . . Is this a man free-associating on his deathbed? Certainly, the hoarse, painful breathing that intersperses the monologue suggests this; so does the ending, which settles Magee's mouth into a hideous, grinning rictus, the frozen sneer of a stone satyr. . . . Late Beckett writes with a grim beauty, using sharp, concentrated, and resonant images of deprivation and anguish to draw attention to the human waste we see all around us, if usually in a less extreme form. What worries me isn't his insistence on this waste, but his apparent belief that there's no point doing anything about it — in a godless universe man might as well withdraw into himself and slowly rot.

> Benedict Nightingale, *New Statesman,* 28 May 1976, p. 723,
> reprinted in *Critical Heritage,* p. 346-8

Like most of Mr. Beckett's plays it deals with the horror of the past. . . . Here is Mr. Magree's voice, prerecorded, through three speakers, sounding less like a circular saw than usual, softened but no more attractive, and decidedly soporific. High on the list of the things which I can live, even die, without would be, had I ever thought of it, Mr. Magee in three-track stereo. Faber and Faber, in the blurb to the published version, say of Magee and Magee and Magee: 'The voices speak of the past; nostalgic, regretful, elegiac, poignant, fragmentary'. The adjectives are not really deniable, and I might have used a couple of them myself. But the substance is only a rerun of *Krapp's Last Tape* without the props: a process of refinement but not necessarily of enrichment.

> Robert Cushman, *The Observer,* 23 May 1976, p. 30
> reprinted in *Critical Heritage,* p. 343-4

Tuesday, 31 Aug. 1976. Beckett defines first of all the function of the three loudspeakers. They are supposed to make the transition from one story to another clear. It is the same voice but the stories are taking place at different levels of time. The voices flow without serious interruption into one another and are only differentiated by the position of the loudspeakers on the left, in the middle, and on the right of the eight-foot-high platform on which the man is sitting. . . .
Friday, 3 Sept. 1976. The B story is the most emotional, the C story however is cold, almost cynical. . . . Beckett demonstrates the speaking himself: flat, inaudibly breathing, murmuring,

dreamy, without any noticeable interruption, he goes through a whole speech without stopping. . . .

Thursday, 16 Sept. 1976. Beckett comments on the silence after each of the three parts: in these moments the man comes back to the present. While he was listening to his voice he was in the past. . . . During the listening everything is closed, in the silence he is startled to find himself in the present, everything is open. . . . Finally, he says, half jokingly, he can't bear the text any more . . . he is completely impregnated with it. . . . We make the recording without him.

Walter D. Asmus, trans. Helen Watanabe, rehearsal notes for the German premiere of Beckett's *That Time* and *Footfalls* at the Schiller Th., Werkstatt, Berlin, in *Journal of Beckett Studies,* No. 2 (Summer 1977), p. 92-94

In the vanishing landscape ruin is superimposed on ruin; the man seeking the crumbling tower where the child played takes his way by the boarded-up Doric terminus of the Great Southern and Eastern, with its crumbling colonnade. This is Time the destroyer, reducing everything to rubble and dust. But the great recurring phrase from which the play takes its title is not 'Time' but 'That time', a very different thing; 'That time' — when we did this or that, remembered this and that; times the mind dwells on, delights in evoking; times good and not so good, times that Time has not taken along with the trams, the places, the physical presence of the loved ones. . . . Stops and starts of the mind; something is always there, sifting, getting the scenes right; it is an active, creative process. . . . All phases are seen in retrospect, 'that time' glimpsed through another, layers upon layers of a life, not finally to be separated; the far-off child no less — and no more — vivid than the man seeking the place where the child was, the decrepit character in the green coat with his needless nightbag. Any time may have moments of high intensity: it is out of old age that the voice draws a transcendent experience which was for us in the theatre a moment of great haunting beauty. . . . Youth and age run together in the end, unity asserts itself over separateness. . . . The words have mournful undertones of gravestone and morgue, but always too they are associated with continuance and creativity; the child's marvellous inventive power, the old man's tenacity, searching for ways 'out'.

Katherine J. Worth, 'Review Article: Beckett's Fine Shades', *Journal of Beckett Studies,* No. 1 (Winter 1976), p. 76-7

Footfalls

Play in one act.
Written: in English, 1975; *translated* into French as *Pas* by
    Beckett.
First London production: Royal Court Th., 20 May 1976 (dir.
    Beckett; with Billie Whitelaw).
First American production: Arena Stage, Kreeger Th., Washington,
    D.C., Dec. 1976 (dir. Alan Schneider).
Revived: Samuel Beckett Th., New York, 14 Feb. 1984 (dir.
    Alan Schneider).
Published: New York: Grove Press, 1976; Paris: Éditions de
    minuit, 1977; and in *Ends and Odds*.

*Footfalls is a dialogue between May (Beckett's mother's name)
and May's mother, whose voice we hear, but whom we never see.
The mother is bedridden; May, who never leaves the house, looks
after her. But the most striking aspect of the play is May's pacing
– the footfalls across a narrow lighted strip of the stage (Beckett
specifies nine steps, width one metre, in his stage directions). The
mother tells us that May has always paced since she was a little
girl; they removed the carpet because she 'must hear the feet,
however faint they fall'. She spends each sleepless night walking
and mulling over 'it all'. After a pause and blackout, May resumes
with a 'sequel', the story of Mrs. Winter and her daughter Amy,
who paced up and down in the little village church. The characters
are obviously the same even though the names are unaccountably
altered. May ends by quoting Amy's mother: 'Will you never have
done ... revolving it all?* [Pause] *It?* [Pause] *It all.* [Pause] *In
your poor mind.* [Pause] *It all.'*

The last play seems almost to belong to a different genre. It is
eerie and seems to tell a story. In *Footfalls,* a middle-aged woman
(though she grows older), dressed in a Miss Haversham film of
folds, paces up and down, nine steps to the right, nine to the left.
She is listening to the presence of her mother, reduced to a patch
of ectoplasm, in the deep, dark recesses of her mind. Guilts,
memories of loss, and the sheer daily troubles of the world keep
the woman to her treadmill, as she ages, but becomes less capable
of even being born, as a separate person. The ties of an endless
childhood, stretching on to a premature senility, have never been

51

so graphically and compellingly expressed.
John Elsom, *The Listener,* 27 May 1976, p. 681
reprinted in *Critical Heritage,* p. 346

Both plays *[Footfalls* and *That Time]* are interior monologues.
The words seem to tumble directly from the subconscious. They
seem disoriented, but, listening, wafted on a lyrical tide of images,
we find an order and a poetry. Each play is a litany of remem-
brance.
Mel Gussow, *New York Times,* 26 Dec. 1976, Sec. II, p.22

[Jim Knowlson] Can we move on now to *Footfalls,* put on in
1976, and written especially for you by Samuel Beckett. . . . I remember noting at the time at rehearsal Beckett's remark to Rose
Hill about the production, 'We are not trying to do this play
realistically or psychologically but musically'. This was an element,
presumably, that you must have concentrated rather a lot upon at
rehearsal?

[Billie Whitelaw] Yes, this is something that happens. When I was
doing *Not I,* I felt . . . like an athlete crashing through barriers,
but also like a musical instrument playing notes. . . . In *Footfalls,*
I felt like a moving musical Edvard Munch painting — one felt like
all three — and in fact when Beckett was directing *Footfalls,* he
was not only using me to play the notes, but I almost felt that he
did have the paintbrush out and was painting, and, of course,
what he always has in the other pocket is the rubber, because as
fast as he draws a line in, he gets out that enormous india-rubber
and rubs it out until it is only faintly there.
'Extracts from an unscripted interview with Billie Whitelaw
by James Knowlson, a television recording made 1 Feb. 1977,
in *Journal of Beckett Studies,* No. 3 (Summer 1978), p. 89

Footfalls is also about separation and unity though more obliquely
and oddly: for one or two reviewers it remained an unreadable
mystery, though all agreed, as surely they had to, on the extraordinary spellbinding quality of Billie Whitelaw as the daughter.
Surrounded by darkness, in silence broken only by the sound of
her own footfalls, she created one of Beckett's most overwhelming
visual images; a sculptured figure of tragic grandeur, in her trailing
robe, dimly grey in the dim light, painfully bowed, arms crossed
over breast, pacing her nine rhythmic steps to and fro on the

narrow strip of stage she is confined to. A terribly exposed, solitary role, such as the actress of *Not I* could do, but how few besides; Beckett wrote it as her play and in her performance she made it so. . . . The second sequence, like the first, ends with the mother contemplating what the daughter endures: she fades away on the thought of all the pain. . . . There is a suggestion here of suffering not confined to the two of them: it widens out in the mind, as the echoes spread out from the chime.

Katherine J. Worth, 'Review Article: Beckett's Fine Shades',
Journal of Beckett Studies, No. 1 (Winter 1976), p. 78-9

Time past is always Beckett's concern. Time past as a monument. Time past as a record that we were once there. The transience of a man who does not believe in permanence yet still wants to record his existence. These plays are graffiti on the walls of time.

Clive Barnes, *New York Times,* 10 Dec. 1976

Ghost Trio

Television play.
Written: in English, 1975.
First broadcast: BBC 2, 17 Apr. 1977 (dir. Donald McWhinnie, supervised by Beckett).
Revived: in German, as *Geister-trio,* Süddeutscher Rundfunk, Stüttgart, 1977 (dir. Beckett).
Published: in *Ends and Odds.*

As the title suggests, this brief play is in three segments, with Beethoven's Fifth Piano Trio as accompaniment. The male figure (F) is seen but not heard; the only dialogue issues from a female voice. In Part I, the voice takes the TV camera on a guided tour of the spare grey room – wall, floor, window, dust, finally focusing on a solitary figure seated and holding a cassette. In Part II, the voice informs us that F 'thinks he hears her'. He waits tensely, going twice to the door and once to the window to look out, returning each time to his stool and cassette. In Part III, at the voice's command of 'Repeat', the camera returns to shots of F, waiting and looking, this time with only musical, not verbal accompaniment. At the end, F answers a knock at the door, only to find a small boy, who twice shakes his head, and then departs.

Relax, Martin Esslin advised us, talking to Melvyn Bragg before each play. Relax and surrender to Beckett's spell: it will grow in your mind. There is no doubt that the reductionist scale and austerity of Beckett's late work is effective on the small screen, although the dynamics are pitched so low that if the plays were any longer you might well drop off. The timing of *Ghost Trio* was mesmeric and Donald McWhinnie's direction, in which the camera advanced with tremulous hesitancy on the actor (Ronald Pickup) like a camera in the prehistoric days of moving films, created a world out of time and space.

> Michael Ratcliffe, *The Times,* 18 Apr. 1977, p. 6
> reprinted in *Critical Heritage,* p. 353

Although the text opens with the voice giving explicit television directions . . . so making explicit at once that this is consciously a TV script, the logic of television itself is emphasized by the voice's stress on its lack of inflexion. . . . For, of course, the television camera is simply an expressionless eye, and Beckett goes out of his way to keep the viewer aware of this absence of inflexion, interpretation, and camera commentary. . . . The stress on greyness and the absence of shadows still further, and deliberately underline Beckett's minimal use of the television camera: for the camera just sees, and everything else . . . is interpretation and is consciously planned by the director as the artist. The stress on the *artist* leads us to one of the central secrets of this play, that Beckett is calling on the resources of all the arts, and presenting a critique of what they can and cannot achieve (the poet is represented by the presence of words; the novelist by the presence of plot and narrative; the dramatist by the presence of dramaturgical devices; the composer by the reliance on music; the television director by the very medium of *Ghost Trio's* presentation; the painter by the handling of the visual devices; the photographer by the presence of grey colouring and the still figure framed in the lens of the still-life picture). . . . The very title, *Ghost Trio* (as with Strindberg's *Ghost Sonata,* or Tolstoy's *Kreutzer Sonata*) takes up the metaphor of the *artist* as musician, precisely punning on 'The Ghost' trio by Beethoven, the tripartite division of the play, and the three 'ghostly' characters themselves. But what is especially significant, the text makes clear, is that there is no automatic linking of the music which we hear and the cassette which the man is holding. . . . Beckett's *Ghost Trio* is thus a profound reflection on the atmosphere and the potency of one particular motif from the second movement of Beethoven's trio, employing the music both to counterpoint the dramatic action and to crystallize his assumptions about the *artist* and especially the differing status of the individual arts.

Fletcher, *et. al., Student's Guide* p. 212-15

Ghost Trio is composed entirely in units of three and seems to have three objects: to reduce as always the human condition to a simple definition in terms of new allegory; to give the academics a good puzzle to solve; and thirdly to make some wry personal statements about the author himself and his own past work and present situation. The play itself is conceived within three frames, each containing another frame and another world like a Chinese box. The outer frame is that of the television screen itself. . . . The voice of a woman announcer, that of Billie Whitelaw, operates on this plane, explaining what is seen in the second frame, that of the visual narrative. The third plane is interior, that of the inside of the mind of the protagonist and of the music. . . . The announcer's voice . . . describes three of the rectangular objects that can be seen, a door, a window, and a pallet or simple bed on the floor. . . . I take these to represent in the author's mind, birth, copulation, and death; the door (entry) being birth, the window (which shows teeming rain outside on a black night — a clear enough sexual image) procreation, and the pallet (coffin shaped . . .) death. . . . But he also makes sly allusions to his past dramatic work: the boy instantly conjured up both *Waiting for Godot* and *Endgame:* the face in the mirror brings back *Film* and *Eh Joe;* the music, which comes and goes, the sound effects, the narrator's voice, all belong to the world of the radio plays.

John Calder, 'Review', *Journal of Beckett Studies,* No. 2 (Summer 1977), p. 117-19

'. . . but the clouds . . .'

Television play.
Written: in English, 1976.
First broadcast: BBC TV, 17 Apr. 1977 (dir. Donald McWhinnie).
Published: in *Ends and Odds*

Like Ghost Trio, *with which it appeared, this play features a man waiting for a woman. He walks the roads from dawn to night, or so his disembodied voice tells us, coming home to his 'little sanctum' and silently begging her to appear. M's voice posits four possibilities, each briefly enacted by the figures who silently appear from the shadows surrounding the circular set: 1) she appeared and 'in the same breath was gone'; 2) she appeared and lingered briefly; 3) she appeared and spoke to him before vanishing; or 4) by far the most common, she did not appear, and he was merely left wishing for her until, at dawn, he again took his solitary figure wandering the roads again.*

Both new plays share a kinship with *Godot,* each show a man waiting, hoping, listening for the memory and return of a woman once loved. . . . In the second play . . . a man in black walks into a pool of light and out of it the other side to reemerge in a white robe. He retires to a sanctum at the back to conjure again the vision of his speaking love (this time we see her face). These movements are repeated several times and if you are hooked – it is less immediately impressive than *Ghost Trio* – it is partly because you know what is coming next.

Michael Ratcliffe, *The Times,* 18 Apr. 1977, p. 6

The title . . . comes from Yeat's moving description of the deprivations of old age in his poem 'The Tower', when all that is left is intellect, work and study, and when the slowing of the body is a minor nuisance compared to worse evils:

The death of friends, or death
Of every brilliant eye
That made a catch in the breath –
Seem but the clouds of the sky
When the horizon fades . . .

The play makes its own comment on age, memory, and nostalgia with economy, and with one strictly controlled camera-angle and field of vision. . . . Both the television plays belong to the new Beckett whose work has developed an equanimity reminiscent of Cicero and Goethe, as well as Yeats. It would be too much to say that the agony and cruelty of the early and middle work has disappeared, but there is now a mellow acceptance of the inevitable, a poetry of comfort, projected with ever greater precision. Best of all, Mr. Beckett is no longer trapped in a tunnel of his own making, but exploring a seam full of endless possibilities, without ever having once left the straight path, inevitable as it now seems, of his own very personal view of life and art, and economy of style and expression.

John Calder, 'Review', *Journal of Beckett Studies,* No. 2
(Summer 1977), p. 120

A Piece of Monologue

Dramatic monologue.
Written: in English, 1979.
First American production: La Mama E.T.C., New York City,
    Dec. 1979 (dir. David Warrilow).
Published: London: Faber and Faber, 1982; and in *The Kenyon
    Review,* New Series, I, iii (Summer 1979).

*This monologue is spoken by an old man, dressed in white night-
gown and socks, in the dead of night, stage dimly lit. The opening
sentence sets both the tone and theme for the piece: 'Birth was
the death of him'. Presumably the speaker, though the subject is
always referred to in the third person, the old man has gone 'from
funeral to funeral' two and a half billion seconds until now. Every
night he awakens, lights the lamp, and stands facing a blank wall,
blank except for a few pins which once held up the pictures of –
he cannot quite say 'loved ones'. Picture by picture, he tore them
from the wall and ripped them up. His memory keeps returning
to the funeral of a woman: 'Rain pelting. Umbrellas round a
grave. Seen from above. Streaming black canopies. Black ditch
beneath'. He returns his mind to the room: 'Ghost light, Ghost
room. Ghost grave'. He is utterly alone, himself nearly a ghost.*

The play is called *A Piece of Monologue,* and it was written by
Beckett especially for Mr. Warrilow, who is performing the work
in its world premiere in the Annex at La Mama. The monologue
lasts 50 minutes. It is a dead-of-night soliloquy, an elegy to the
brevity of life and the proximity of death . . . exegesis is super-
fluous. In common with other, later plays by Beckett, *A Piece of
Monologue* is a study in mood and tempo. Character is sacrificed
to temperature. We cannot name the Speaker – he may be one
man or all men – although necessarily one concludes that he is a
representation of the author. The image is the essence. The beat
is inexorable. . . . The play is short and dense . . . and one might
justifiably ask, what advantage is there in seeing it rather than
reading it? On paper, it is a poem. Performed, it breathes; the
actor gives it dramatic texture. With his bony, Giacometti-like
form and his eloquent voice, Mr. Warrilow . . . is a quintessential
Beckett actor. . . . *A Piece of Monologue* is a spellbinding visitation
from an artist's subconscious.
    Mel Gussow, *New York Times,* 19 Dec. 1979, Sec. C, p. 32-4

Rockaby

Play in one act.
Written: in English, 1981.
First production: Center for Theatre Research in Buffalo, New
   York, 8 Apr. 1981 (dir. Alan Schneider; with Billie Whitelaw).
First London production: National Th., at the Cottesloe, Dec.
   1982.
Revived: Samuel Beckett Th., New York, 16 Feb. 1984 (dir.
   Alan Schneider).
First television production: BBC 2, 15 Dec. 1982.
Published: New York: Grove Press, 1981; London: Faber and
   Faber, 1982

In Rockaby, *the sole figure on the stage is an old woman dressed
in a black, lacy, high-necked evening gown. Her sole activity is
rocking slowly in a wooden rocker, 'highly polished to gleam
when rocking'. She speaks only one word – 'more' – but each
time, she prompts her recorded voice in poetic phrases to tell of
a woman (either herself or, suggested later, her mother) who
spent her days looking for 'another like herself', searching until*
'time she stopped'. *Each of the four sections of the play reduces
the woman's hopes as she sits at her window, looking out on
other windows, still searching for another like herself, then, at
last, only for another window like her own. In the end, she lowers
the blind, rocking and waiting for death; 'let down the blind and
stopped/time she went down/down the steep stair/time she went
right down/was her own other/own other living soul'. Eyes closed,
having given up, she rocks rhythmically to her own despairing
words: 'rock her off/stop her eyes/fuck life/stop her eyes/rock
off/rock her off'.*

If the play didn't have Beckett's name attached, you might have
taken it for a prequel to *Psycho:* when was Anthony Perkins
going to come on and kiss his old mum goodbye? But it is Beckett,
of course, and Arena's academics and theatre-folk invited us to
assume the traditional posture: kneeling on all fours with a bag
over our head. ... You can argue this line as a gradual process of
refinement, of discarding artifice, reaching down into the ele-
mental, turning language into incantation, and laying bare the
essential human condition in one stark metaphor after another.

But you can also see it as a process in which the full resources of language are rebuffed, interest in character is discarded, humour is reined in, and the actor becomes merely the vehicle for a prose text. First the eggs of drama are blown, and then all the eggshells are put in one basket.

Julian Barnes, *The Observer,* 19 Dec. 1982, p. 36

The fact that Beckett writes plays for Billie Whitelaw to star in is one of the few completely comprehensible things about him. ... In the case of *Rockaby* Beckett has provided his actress with a particularly beautiful solo: the memory-cum-threnody of an old woman who is rocking herself into the sleep of death. It I had to christen the genre, I'd call it a crone-poem. Internally overlapping and repeating itself like a system of mingled villanelles, this calming lyric of senility was given an unbeatable mellifluous and rhythmical reading by Miss Whitelaw — for whom the whole experience must be a relative doddle, given that she does have a chair to sit in, and that most of the performance is pre-recorded on tape.

Russell Davies, *Sunday Times,* 19 Dec. 1982, p. 40

Rockaby is one more of Beckett's border crossings. Conceive of the crossing from life to death as a border between countries; conceive, too, that it is possible to see across before going, to float above the border a bit, and to itemize one's final hopes and hopelessness, memories and bitterness, and joy and relief, as if in a customs declaration done in the form of a laconic poem. ... Its delicate cumulative quality, its oboe-like winding toward the revelation of absolute loneliness, the shock of the consequent obscene renunciation of existence, the end of rocking felt as the end of her pulse — all these I discerned from the printed page. None of these subtle beauties is achieved or even outlined in the performance directed by Schneider. ... It's all blind Beckett worship, not acute Beckett performance.

Stanley Kauffmann, *Saturday Review,* June 1981, p. 62-3

Ohio Impromptu

Play in one act.
Written: in English, 1980.
First American production: Ohio State University, 9 May 1981,
 trans. to Harold Clurman Th., New York, May 1983 (dir. Alan

Schneider; with David Warrilow).
Published: in *Rockaby and Other Short Pieces* (Grove Press, 1981).

The stage-picture is memorable. Two figures, both clad in black, with long white hair which hides their faces from the audience, sit on white chairs at adjacent sides of a white table. The only prop is an authentically Joycean 'old world Latin Quarter hat'. The two figures are identical in appearance, differing only in function: one is a reader, the 'book on table before him open at last pages', *the other a listener. The story read out from his book by the Reader begins with the 'last attempt' made by a man to 'obtain relief' after the loss of a 'dear one'. For his swan song he moves into a single room with a view of 'the Isle of Swans'.... But the 'dear face' had warned him in a dream against the move he has made ... and his 'old terror of night' returns. One night a man appears to him, announces himself sent by the dear one, takes a worn volume from his coat pocket, sits down, reads until dawn, and then disappears. This comfort continues 'from time to time' until 'with never a word exchanged they grew to be as one'. One night the man does not disappear as usual but announces, 'I saw the dear face and heard the unspoken words. No need to go to him again, even were it in your power'. ... The 'sad tale' at the end of the book tells, then, of loss, suffering, and reconciliation, the last perhaps in death. ... Throughout the piece the Listener not only listens but also regulates his companion's reading by knocking on the table with his left hand. ... He is ordering the reading in such a way as to ensure that this will be the final telling of the tale.*

Paul Lawley, *Theatre Journal,* XXXIII (Oct. 1981)

Throughout this play, perhaps fifteen minutes long, the logically impossible recurs. The book contains a story of past, present, and future. It describes completed actions as it preordains them. Visual and verbal pictures cross and create afterimages of each other. One senses an infinite circularity to the narrative, yet it comes to an inevitable end. Time catches up with what is written. This paradoxical conflation of narrative past tense and dramatic presence is the theatricality of *Ohio Impromptu:* only theatre can present this tension of action completing itself, time running out, leaving characters posed immovably between memory and will, astride the grave.

Alisa Solomon, *Village Voice,* 28 June 1983, p. 99-100

Quad

'Ballet for four people' for television.
First production: as *Quadrat 1+2,* Süddeutscher Rundfunk, 1982.
First English production: BBC 2, 16 Dec. 1982.
Published: London: Faber and Faber, 1984.

Quad *consists of a wordless series of movements within a square for four players, 'as alike in build as possible'. Each player wears a different coloured gown reaching to the floor, and a cowl which hides his face. The camera remains fixed, as each player enters and completes his series of triangular courses, and is then joined by another. Beckett designates four possible solos, six possible duos, and four possible trios, all to percussion instruments. The total playing time is approximately 25 minutes.*

Somehow, the wrong sort of abstractness was emphasized [in] *Quad,* the wordless play where hooded figures like preoccupied Capuchins criss-cross a small square of floor, never quite meeting in the middle or indeed anywhere else. After a while, this begins to look like a TV game, idling away in a shop window. One missed the sense of being imprisoned in a theatrical darkness, getting tortured along with Beckett's actors, those virtuosi in chirpy suffering.

Russell Davies, *Sunday Times,* 19 Dec. 1982, p. 40

Four caped and hooded figures silently patrolled a square stage: first along the sides, then across the diagonals, but always avoiding the central area which contained a large black dot (was it, perhaps, a punning animation of the way in which man is forever 'missing the point'?) This went on for a while in colour with percussion backing, then switched to monochrome with shuffling feet. Martin Esslin gamely called the piece 'funny' in his introduction, and remarked, 'Who else but Samuel Beckett dare experiment like this?' More to the point, who else would get such a work put on? One of the percussionists in this Stuttgart production, I noticed, was called Rubik. Perhaps there is a clue for us all here.

Julian Barnes, *The Observer,* 19 Dec. 1982, p. 36

Catastrophe

Play in one act.
Written: in French, 1982.
First production: Avignon Festival, 1982.
First American production: Harold Clurman Th., New York,
June 1983 (dir. Alan Schneider; with David Warrilow).
Published: Paris: Éditions de minuit, 1982; London: Faber and
Faber, 1984; and in *The New Yorker,* 10 Jan. 1983.

Written for Vaclav Havel, the dissident Czech playwright who has been jailed for his outspokenness on human rights issues, Catastrophe *takes place in a theatre. Here The Director and his Assistant prepare their 'catastrophe' for an upcoming exhibition: they mould the Protagonist (David Warrilow) into martyrdom. Dressed in an unmistakably Russian fur hat and coat, the Director sits in an armchair and barks orders at his obedient Assistant. The Protagonist stands on a pedestal, shivering slightly. They strip him down, change his posture, and consider their work. When the Director calls for more flesh, his Assistant removes the Protagonist's black coat to reveal grey pajamas. She opens his collar, rolls his pants legs above his knees, and, on further orders, removes his hands from his pockets and joins them in near-prayer position at his breast. Warrilow, again, is superb as the submissive, sacrificial statue, bereft of speech and identity – Beckett's unaccommodated man. Impatient to get to a caucus, the Director puffs on a cigar and bombastically rejects his Assistant's suggestion that they put a gag on the Protagonist. 'This craze for explication!' he cries. 'Every i dotted to death! Little gag! For God's sake!'. . . To complete his creation, the Director wants light focused tightly on the Protagonist, then to focus on his head alone. In this light, with a soundtrack of distant applause, the Protagonist raises his head and gazes steadily at the audience. After a pause, the lights fade slowly, leaving a haunting, skull-like image. With its Christian overtones,* Catastrophe *is a political miracle play. Luke might record the sacrifice of this figure, stripped, silenced, and de-*
62

humanized.
Alisa Solomon, *Village Voice,* 28 June 1983, p. 100

As often with Beckett, there is a kind of black humour even in the grimmest of subjects: since the Protagonist is continually being given orders by a theatrical producer, the play can be seen both as a kind of parody of agit prop plays as well as a statement of the similarity between a dictatorship (whether of the proletariat or not) and the way in which a director treats his actors.
Richard Roud, *Manchester Guardian Weekly,* 21 Aug. 1983, p. 20

At the end, after some orders shouted by an unseen light man, Protagonist stands on a dark stage with only a spotlight on his frightened face. Director predicts an enthusiastic response from the audience; a sound effect of applause follows, in which I thought I also heard hoofbeats and the turning wheels of a tumbrel — but maybe not, maybe that was only an aural hallucination from my own spellbound imagination. ... Even without the dedication, the political implications are clear.
Edith Oliver, *The New Yorker,* 27 June 1983, p. 75

Nacht und Träume

Television play.
Written: in German, 1982.
First production: Süddeutscher Rundfunk, 19 May 1983.
Published: in *Collected Shorter Plays.*

Nacht und Träume *is a wordless play, the only sound that of a male voice first humming, then singing, from the last seven bars of Schubert's* 'Lied, Nacht, und Träume'. *The only character in a dimly lit room is a man, the Dreamer (A), grey-haired, seated at a table. As he rests his head on his hands, his 'Dreamt Self' (B) becomes visible. Dreamt hands appear from above, touching B's head, extending a cup for him to drink, wiping his brow. The dreamt self gazes upward, joins hands with the dreamt hands. These hands are all lowered to the table to serve as a rest for B's head. The dream fades as the light focuses again on the original Dreamer; then the dream is repeated again more slowly before all the figures fade away.*

One would have to see this production to know whether the prevailing impression is of loneliness or of comfort. The visual effects as described in the text and Schubert's music, which is highly melodic, would suggest beauty and peacefulness. But again, Beckett presents us with a solitary, aged figure. One thinks of the woman in *Rockaby* who, unable to find any other like herself, 'time she went right down/was her own other/own other living soul'. Consistently Beckett has presented in his plays two incomplete characters who together make up a whole (blind Hamm and Clov in *Endgame,* for example, or Music and Voice in the radio plays), but in his latest plays such as *What Where,* which contain more than one character, the *doppelgänger* is more directly a twin (Reader and Listener look as exactly alike as possible). Further, in *What Where,* as in *Nacht und Träume,* the *doppelgänger* serves as a comforter, as though to imply that the aged man has found peace with himself.

What Where

Play in one act.
Written: in English, 1983.
First production: Harold Clurman Th., New York, 15 June 1983 (dir. Alan Schneider).
Published: Faber and Faber, 1984.

Like Catastrophe, What Where ... *takes up the world's woes. In this darker, thicker play, four barely distinguishable figures (Bam, Bom, Bim, and Bem) repeat a pattern of action a number of times. They all have long grey hair and wear ragged grey gowns. In turn, each figure appears to Bam on the dim stage. Bam asks about the results of an interrogation: 'He didn't say anything? You gave him the works? He wept? Screamed? Begged for mercy? But didn't say anything?' The answer is always no. Bam does not believe this, and calls on the next figure to take the first one off and make him confess 'that he said it to him'. Each figure interrogates the next. Each receives no answer. This pattern repeats itself again and again. The first time there is no dialogue, the Voice of Bam continues to narrate, often interrupting the actual Bam with 'Not good. I start again'. The actual Bam starts his questions again with slight variation.*

Schneider has said that he sees Bam, Bom, Bim, and Bem as successive generations of men trying, with continual desperation and failure, to understand the what and where of existence. He considers 'the works' to be the great works of philosophy — Plato, Aristotle, Hegel, and so on. But I take *What Where* more literally, even more bleakly: 'the works' as torture under the anonymous power of the Voice or Bam. This voice is represented by a megaphone, perched downstage right, its larger circular end facing front, lit so the center is black, but the rim illuminated — like a fully eclipsed moon. It is frightening. Even though the Voice is Bam's it is a strangely disembodied, separate authority. And it counts as a single entity: 'We are the last five', the play begins. This detached speaker is quite different from those in *That Time, A Piece of Monologue, Not I,* and *Rockaby* — this one uses the first person. This voice, an omnipotent, totalitarian image, is the only one with an ego. As usual, these Beckett plays cannot be summed up in any statement of theme. The images seem somehow preconscious; they are resonant and haunting. At the end of *What Where* Bam's Voice suggests, 'Make sense who may'.

Alisa Soloman, *Village Voice,* 28 June 1983, p. 100

The last play, *What Where,* also has political implications. It should not be forgotten that Beckett was a Resistance hero, a signatory of the 121 Petition against the Algerian war, not some ivory-tower hermetic figure who has nothing to do with the world in which we live. Again, like *Catastrophe,* it is a play about totalitarianism, complete with a Grand Inquisition and four characters. ... But the Grand Inquisitor is identified in the programme as the 'Voice of Bam': often we are ouselves our own Grand Inquisitors. The play concludes with the words 'make sense who may', but this is no haughty disclaimer. We can — indeed we must — understand self-imposed tyranny, or worse luck for us. What I find extraordinary is that all the New York critics, even those one sometimes thinks of as philistines, have acclaimed [these] plays. Snobbery? Fashion? The Nobel Prize? I don't think so. As Auden reminded us years ago, we all worship language, and I do not think there is anyone alive who writes English (and French) as well as Samuel Beckett. And Beckett proves once again that he can say as much in fifteen minutes as anyone else can in two hours. Less is more.
Richard Roud, *Manchester Guardian Weekly,* 21 Aug. 1983, p. 20

a: Prose in Performance

Ever since Jack MacGowran put together a one-man
show of selections from Beckett's prose in 1962, the
dramatic possibilities inherent in his prose writings
have appealed to numerous actors and directors. There
remain few prose pieces which have not been staged or
broadcast in some fashion − this despite the author's
own statement that, as a rule, works should be presented
in the medium for which they were written. In this
section, the arrangement is chronological by date of first
performance, not in order of writing or publication.

End of Day
One-man show, adapted by Jack MacGowran with
    Beckett's assistance.
First production: Gaiety Th., Dublin, 5 Oct. 1962;
    trans. to New Arts Th., London, 16 Oct. 1962.
Recorded: Claddagh Records, 1966 (supervised by
    Beckett, accompanied by Edward Beckett on flute,
    John Beckett on harmonium, and Beckett himself
    on the gong).

*At first MacGowran intended to do straight readings,
but . . . he developed a different idea: . . . 'a composite
character of the intellectual tramp, and this became
my central figure. I began with Molloy: "I shall soon
be quite dead at last" . . . and then he goes on to his
reminiscences of his father, his mother, his youth, his
experience, how he finds no answers, the moments of
happiness, the humour, the double vision of tragedy
and comedy, because these after all are closely allied
and Beckett saw them at one and the same time. . . .
The key word in my show is one I think is the key
word in all Beckett's writings:* perhaps.' *. . . Beckett
was responsible for the costume MacGowran wore: a
very old, too-large overcoat, ragged at the bottom,
dirty and black, held together with a large pin. He
also wore a grimy scarf, a tattered brown handkerchief,
a pair of old beat-up work shoes several sizes too large,
trousers too short and no socks. . . . Simplicity was*
66

the keynote of the setting and the interpretation as well: 'Beckett told me that when I came to a passage with several meanings, the obvious one is the right one. He told me he did not create symbols where they did not exist, only where they are apparent.'

Dierdre Bair, *Samuel Beckett*, p. 467-8

From Beginning to End
One-man show assembled by Jack MacGowran from
  Beckett's prose.
First production: on tour in the United States, 1968-69.
Revived: with *Happy Days,* Schiller Th., Berlin, 1971.
Broadcast: BBC TV, 'Monitor', 23 Feb. 1965.

From an Abandoned Work
Written: in English, 1954.
Performed: Shivaun O'Casey, on tour in the United States, 1963.
Published: London: Faber and Faber, 1958.

I feel also that no form of monologue technique will work for this text and that it should somehow be presented as a document for which the speaker is not responsible. ... What would you think of the following set up? Moonlight, Ashcan a little left of centre. Enter man left, limping, with stick, shadowing in paint general lighting along. Advances to can, raises lid, pushes about inside with crook of stick, inspects and rejects (puts back in can) an unidentifiable refuse, fishes out finally tattered ms. or copy of FAAW, reads aloud standing – 'Up bright and early that day, I was young then, feeling awful, and out' – and a little further in silence, lowers texts, stands motionless, finally closes ashcan, sits down on it, hooks stick round neck, and reads text through from beginning. ... Finishes, sits a moment motionless, gets up, replaces text in ashcan, and limps off right. ... If you like this idea, you'll be able to improve on it. But keep it cool.

Beckett, letter to Shivaun O'Casey, 1 Apr. 1963,
quoted by Deirdre Bair, *Samuel Beckett*, p. 487-8

Imagination Dead Imagine

Written: in French as *Imagination morte imaginez.*
Recorded: BBC, 1966, with Jack MacGowran.
Published: Paris: Éditions de minuit, 1965; London: Calder
  and Boyars, 1965.

Imagination Dead Imagine *creates an image of a small white rotunda, three feet in height and in diameter, rising from a flat white plain, in which two bodies, male and female, lie back to back in the foetal position. Light comes and goes, being succeeded by intervals of freezing cold and absolute darkness. The bodies are alive, as may be seen by holding a mirror in front of their lips and from the fact that the left eyes open at intervals and 'gaze in unblinking exposure long beyond what is humanly possible'. The key sentence, in terms of what may be discerned about Mr. Beckett's themes from the rest of his work, appears to be the ironic first: 'No trace of life anywhere, you say, pah, no difficulty there, imagination not dead yet, yes, good, imagination dead imagine'.*

Times Literary Supplement, 30 June 1966, p. 570

Molloy

Written: in French, 1947-49 (see *The Trilogy,* p. 80 below).
Adapted for performance: by E.T. Kirby, *c* 1968.

Kirby has himself summarized his adaptation of Beckett's novel: 'The staged presentation, with the exception of the prologue, was derived entirely from the second or Moran section of the novel. ... First conversational scenes were selected and the dialogue extracted from these scenes, then passages of narrative were selected to be used as such'. ... Thus, the performance was compartmentalized into dramatic units connected by narrative units into both of which technological devices were introduced. ... Live performers played Moran, his son Jacques, and Gaber, who was masked. Molloy and a Figure appeared only on slides and film.

Ruby Cohn, *Just Play,* p. 219-20

The Unnamable
Written: in French, 1949-50 (see *The Trilogy,* p. 80 below).
Adapted for performance: by the American Contemporary Th.,
   1972 (dir. Joseph Dunn and Irja Koljonen).

The programme note to the ACT Unnamable *suggests: 'Time,
light, sound and design values as well as their effects are content
and explicate the event as process and object'. In performance,
the audience sits on four sides of a square playing area, behind a
triple trough of footlights. At the center is a hollow cylinder nine
feet high and nine feet in diameter; a large oval window permits a
view of the interior. After a few minutes of total darkness, the
eyes discern a dim light in the cylinder, which begins to rotate
clockwise with its barely visible human content, the 'I' of Beckett's*
Unnamable. ... *The 'I' speaks nothing but Beckett's words –
about one-fifth of his text in two and three-quarter hours. ... As
the 'I' peers around him and guesses at his surroundings, so does
the audience in the dim light; shadows, phantoms, figures –
'they' – momentarily appear at various points of the room, not
only the playing area. ... The piece uses six actors ... ten light
circuits, recordings of a Moog synthesizer whose playback requires
eight speakers and six tape recorders and amplifiers.*

Ruby Cohn, *Just Play,* p. 222-3

The Lost Ones
Written: in French, as *Le Dépeupleur,* 1966-70.
Adapted for performance: by Mabou Mines, New York City, 1972
   (dir. Lee Breuer, with David Warrilow).
Published: Paris: Éditions de minuit, 1971; London: Calder and
   Boyars, 1972; New York: Grove Press, 1972

The Lost Ones *was intended as a reading-demonstration, actor
David Warrilow holding the book as he pointed to a cross-section
of cylinder with its 200-odd inhabitants of tiny dolls, each half
an inch high. ... Beckett's* Lost Ones *narrates the saga of 200
people 'each searching for its lost one', but that search is confused
with another quest – for a mythical exit from their cylinder
above. Moreover, although each of the searchers seeks compul-
sively, their methods differ, and any given individual need not*

69

sustain his method. At any moment, however, the cylinder popu-
lation divides into even multiples. . . . Mabou Mines designer
Thom Cathcart, having scraped the paint off 205 toy German
railroad dolls, conceived the decisively brilliant idea of seating the
live theatre audience in a rubber cylinder environment.

Ruby Cohn, *Just Play*, p. 224-5

In *The Lost Ones* . . . men and women struggle to escape from the
cylinder in which they are enclosed. It consists of a claustrophobic
monologue accompanied by a barely audible Philip Glass score,
and delivered by a tall, thin actor named David Warrilow to a
small audience, itself enclosed in a black plastic-foam-lined
cylindrical room. The actor manipulates tiny figurines and ladders
within a reduced-scale cross-section of the cylinder, using tweezers
to place them in the set within-the-set. The audience is provided
with opera glasses. The smiling narrator – or lecturer – has the
disturbing manner of a doctor describing the clinical progress of
a disease he knows to be incurable. His equivocal compassion
simply aggravates the deathly anxiety of his listeners.

'Mabou Mines: Frozen Moments,' *Le Monde,* 10 Dec. 1978,
translated in *Manchester Guardian Weekly*

Mercier and Camier
Written: in French, 1945
Adapted for performance: by Frederick Neumann, for Mabou
  Mines, New York Shakespeare Festival Public Th., Oct. 1979
  (dir. Frederick Neumann).
Published: Paris: Éditions de minuit, 1970; London: Calder and
  Boyars, 1974; New York: Grove Press, 1974.

Samuel Beckett's novel Mercier and Camier . . . *is in many respects*
a fictional godfather to Waiting for Godot. *Two cronies – the*
tall, bone-thin Mercier and little, fat Camier – cousins to Didi and
Gogo in Godot *– embark on an aimless journey towards some*
unquestioned goal. The novel is a labyrinth, filled with vaudeville
comedy. These are two tramps in mudtime who manage to survive
in what the author regards as a world of 'hospitable chaos'. . .
Wisely, in his adaptation, Mr. Neumann stresses Beckett's words.
The play is faithful to the passages that it uses from the novel,
but it is, necessarily, highly selective. The adapter has simplified

his source, reducing it largely to a dialogue, pruning barflies and passers-by, which, for one thing, sacrifices a great deal of Beckett's boisterous humour. . . . As in the original, the journey is framed as a story told by an omniscient observer. David Warrilow, cast as the storyteller, is seen on tape on a television screen. . . . As with any adaptation, one could question omissions, but it should be emphasized that Mr. Neumann had made a serious, partially successful attempt to theatricalize Mercier and Camier *with fidelity. It is not an easy journey – for the audience as well as the adaptor – but it is one that is clearly worth the effort.*

Mel Gussow, *New York Times,* 26 Oct. 1979, Sec. C, p.3

The Mabour Mines has given *Mercier and Camier* . . . an almost dream-like quality. These two comically sad figures, who have an almost Laurel and Hardy quality, make an extraordinary voyage. . . . The production, with its strange revolving door reflecting shadowy figures, projected from slides, and gauze-covered walls and ramps from which the two 'heroes' converse over the audience's heads, is a magic one. Frederick Neumann, playing Mercier and Bill Raymond, as his sidekick Camier, are both wonderful as the dark comedians in this opaque dramatic exercise.

William A. Raidy, *Plays and Players,* Dec. 1979, p. 36

Lessness

Written: in French, as *Sans,* 1969.
Adapted for performance: by Francis Warner, for the Rohan
Theatre Group, Oxford Playhouse, Mar. 1982 (dir. Lucy Bailey).
Published: Paris: Éditions de minuit, 1969; London: Calder and
Boyars; New York: Grove Press, 1970.

Lessness . . . *consists of sixty sentences, set down in the sequence in which they came out of Beckett's hat, so that the formal arrangement would mime the spiritual mess that the words of the sentences announce – sixty sentences, what's more, that were then set down all over again, in yet another randomized order, thus increasing the high sense of prevailing disorder. . . . And the litany of distress that these repetitive, circling, and circular bits of language comprise could scarcely be grimmer. The scene is characterized by reductions (ruins, grey, pale, little, scattered, ash,*

71

passing light . . .), by absences (void, blackness, out of mind, blank, all gone, vanished dreams), and by negations. . . . Endlessness, endless, issueless, timeless, changelessness: how these words, uttered over and over, bring home the awful conclusion that lessness is a lessening that will lead irresistibly into states of nothingness.

Valentine Cunningham, *Times Literary Supplement,* 5 Mar. 1982

Texts

Including sections from *Texts for Nothing* and *How It Is.*
Adapted for performance: by Joseph Chaikin, Public Th., New
    York, Mar. 1981 (dir. Steven Kent).

Texts for Nothing
Written: in French, as *Nouvelles et Textes pour rien,* 1950.
Published: Paris: Éditions de minuit, 1955; New York: Grove
    Press, 1967.

[These three short stories and thirteen briefer prose pieces are] all fragments of the single epic of which all Beckett writings are ultimately a part: the epic of man's last days on earth, of each man's last days, which in their bareness and dessication become those of every man. The movement is an oscillation between detachment and attachment, between 'into what nightmare thingness am I fallen?' to 'What counts is to be in the world, the posture is immaterial, so long as one is on earth'.

Dorothy Curley, *Library Book Review,* 1967

How It Is

Written: in French, as *Comment c'est,* 1959.
Published: Paris: Éditions de minuit, 1961; London: Calder and
    Boyars, 1964.

It looks as though Beckett had decided, after more than eight years away from the form, that the novel had not, after all, been 'sufficiently assassinated, sufficiently suicided', so he wrote How It Is *in order to finish the job. . . . Each chunk of prose becomes a spasm of blind effort overtaken by exhaustion, while within the paragraphs the prose moves in short phrases gasped brokenly out*

72

by the narrator, each the span of a single breath. . . . Needless to say, there is no plot to speak of. The book is in three parts: before Pim, with Pim, after Pim. Before Pim there is only the speaker dragging his sack remorselessly through the mud and darkness, occasionally eating, occasionally resting. . . . In Part Two he comes up with Pim, another sufferer in the mud. They grapple, arms and legs entwined like a pair of amorous primaeval reptiles, and crawl together for a while. Infinitely slowly . . . they evolve a satisfying Pavlovian relationship of sadist and victim. . . . In Part Three, when Pim moves away at last, the speaker slowly realizes that, despite appearances he is not alone. He in his turn is awaiting Bom who will treat him as he has treated Pim. All of them are part of an infinite number of damned, moving blindly through the mud in a great chain of torment.

A. Alvarez, *Beckett*, p. 70-4

No writer knows more about the bald power of the word than Mr. Beckett, and Mr. Chaikin quickly demonstrates that few actors know more about turning simple words into theatre. With his director, Steven Kent, he has taken the two works . . . and moulded elegant lamentations into dramatic mysteries. Alone on a tilted stage of wooden planks, Mr. Chaikin struts, shuffles, throws himself to the ground, sits upright and holds internal debates, speaking all the parts of his self-examination and even, in a superior voice, narrating the unspoken words. . . . At about an hour, they have the length of the performance judged exactly, and the variations within are musically exact: not likely to convert those who hate Beckett for his bleak determination to endure, but likely to delight those who have responded before.

Ned Chaillet, *The Times,* 19 June 1981

Enough

Written: in French, as *Assez,* 1965.

Adapted for performance: National Th., at the Cottesloe, with
    Rockaby, Dec. 1982 (dir. Alan Schneider; with Billie Whitelaw).
Revived: Harold Clurman Th., New York, Feb. 1984, with
    Rockaby and *Footfalls.*
Published: Paris: Éditions de minuit, 1966; New York: Grove
    Press, 1967.

*The gentleness of Beckett's voice is not in the words, but in the
hypnotic musicality of speech itself. Billie Whitelaw, probably the
theatre's most accomplished surviving explorer of Beckett's
dramatic intentions, sets up a contrapuntal melody to the meeting
of the words through the sweet lulling rhythms of her voice.
Interestingly, she accompanies her performance in* [Rockaby]
with a reading of the Beckett short story, Enough. *There, in
the bawdy concern with another obscure, unnamed human relationship, there is a touch of optimism, or, perhaps, just bodily
contentment. Gesticulating a bit overmuch, Miss Whitelaw none-
theless points up some good jokes, but the real revelation in the
pairing of the story and the play is Beckett's refined mastery of
the theatre.*

Ned Chaillet, *The Times,* 11 Dec. 1982, p. 7

Company
Written: in English, 1977-79; *translated* into French as *Compagnie*
by Beckett.
Broadcast: BBC Radio 3, July 1980 (with Patrick Magee).
Adapted for performance: National Th. at the Cottesloe, Sept.
1980 (dir. John Russell Brown; with Stephen Moore); Mabou
Mines, New York, 1983 (dir. Frederick Neumann and Honora
Ferguson).
Published: London: John Calder, 1980; Paris: Éditions de minuit,
1980

*All by yourself . . . 'A voice comes to one in the dark . . .' and it
says, 'You are on your back in the dark'. . . . Are you in fact
alone? With this question, this uncertainty, we are launched into
Samuel Beckett's* Company *. . . now presented on Radio 3 as a
75-minute reading by Patrick Magee. . . .* Company *alternates
between the two areas of interest indicated by the voice: 'your'
present position supine in the dark and that life which began
when 'you first saw the light on such and such a day'. Scenes
from the life begin in childhood with a walk through streets on a
late summer afternoon. . . . The scenes that follow all seem to
develop the idea here implied of life as utter and essential loneliness. . . . The title, as I understand it, is therefore ironic: there is
no 'company' and if there seems to be, then it is 'devised', a mere*

*wishful thinking. ... If this seems like a bleak conclusion, then –
so I have been led to believe – Beckett himself does not see it in
that light at all: on the contrary, since all is fable and solitude,
then that's that and in such knowledge we can be relatively
cheerful about life: if the weights of imagination are removed,
the notions for example of heaven and hell, rewards and punishment, with which we torment ourselves, then we can be free.*

David Wade, *Times Literary Supplement,* 19 July 1980

In a precisely controlled word-play, the 'voice' discusses the
relative merits of different types of 'company' and tells anecdotes
about boyhood, manhood and old age: 'company' means anything
that interrupts nothingness, even an itch, a hand movement, or
a memory. ... The stage is furnished with two dilapidated
rocking chairs that face each other with a small table and lamp in
between. ... At the rear of the stage are three white, ten-foot
parabolic discs, which look like radar transmitters, facing right
and slightly upward. As the piece begins, three people enter, walk
behind the discs, and turn them to face the stage, creating a
section of dome, which is described later as the character's
location. ... Neumann's characterization adds theatrical detail
to this man, giving visual life to one who contradicts what he says
even as he says it, who speaks for himself 'as of another' because
that pastime is company. Despite an obvious abundance of am-
bition and good thinking, Neumann and Ferguson's *Company*
cannot withstand such independent evaluation. Viewed alone,
as an avant-garde performance distinct from Beckett's career, it
is verbose, unclear and consequently frustrating.

Jonathan Kalb, *Theatre* (Yale), XIV, 3 (Summer/Fall 1983).
p. 68-71

Ill Seen Ill Said
Written: in French, as *Mal vu mal dit.*
Broadcast: BBC Radio 3, Sept. 1982 (with Patrick Magee).
Published: Paris: Éditions de minuit; New York: Grove Press,
    1981; and in *The New Yorker,* 5 Oct. 1981

Ill Seen Ill Said, *a fable or prose-poem, is [Beckett's] latest view
of what it is to be interned and then interred. An old woman, a
widow, moves slowly towards death. It is the evening of her life,*

75

soon to be night. Soon 'this old so dying woman' will no longer be able to leave the cabin which is her abode, to set out on her small journey to the other abode, the tomb of her husband, all the while another consciousness than hers is trying to see her, to see her exactly and to say her exactly. But the best that can be done could never be good enough. Ill seen ill said; poorly observed, and poorly described. How much dignity of mystery remains unviolated even after the most imaginative exploration. When all is said and done. Ill Seen Ill Said *is a feat of simplicity.*

Christopher Ricks, *Sunday Times,* 12 Sept. 1982, p. 36

Patrick Magee's last performance in a work by Beckett . . . before Magee died earlier this year, marks the end of a collaboration where it was easy to think of the voice, gravelly and sinister, as that of Beckett himself. Terror was the feeling he most often seemed bent on arousing. Beckett's is troubled stuff, and Magee's exposition is presumably the correct one, because he found favour with the author. His last part gave him a bleakly beautiful mono-logue as an observer of another corner of Beckett's wretched landscape, a hut with a dying woman. All is lost, as usual.

Paul Ferris, *The Observer,* 7 Nov. 1982, p. 31

Samuel Beckett's extraordinary monologue . . . was the antithesis of every radio drama convention. There were no characters in the usual sense of the word. There was no dialogue. We never learned who the narrator was, we never knew what status to accord his words. What we got was bits of language, free-floating paradoxes, disembodied senses — the fragmentation of the narrative. . . . No point in dissembling: it made damn difficult listening, although it was easier if you simultaneously read it. . . . As usual, it offered a weary, despondent perception of life as ragged and meaningless, from the penumbra 'at the inexistent centre of a formless place', with a woman who seemed on the point of death.

Anne Karpf, *The Listener,* 4 Nov. 1982, p. 29

Worstward Ho
Written: in English.
Broadcast: BBC Radio 3, 4 Aug. 1983 (dir. Ronald Mason; with Norman Rodway).
Published: London: John Calder, 1983.

You soon feel at home with the plot. Scene: a dimly lit void. As in a parody of the Creation . . . a voice says, or missays, what is to be seen. There are four figures, or 'shades': one whom pain forces to stand upright, one who watches with 'clenched staring eyes', and a man and boy, hand in hand, plodding repeatedly into the distance. As words continue to describe the scene, it gets worse, or better, if you agree with the voice that is longing to be gone: 'Naught best. Best worse.' The standing figure has to bend, then kneel, and ends as an old woman crouched over a grave. The watcher loses hands, face, whites of eyes, skin, and ends as a staring hole. The man and boy lose their boots, lose hold of each other's hands, lose the use of their legs, and end up 'legless plodding on': the usual hopeful condition for Beckett's travellers. . . . Contradicting this self-parodically nihilistic plot is a low creeping form of energetic half-life oozing . . . .into every sentence.

Hermione Lee, *The Observer,* 22 May 1983, p. 30

There is an element of strangeness in the work of Samuel Beckett which always challenges the listener's acceptance, but hearing *Worstward Ho* it occurred to me that that strangeness may here have been somewhat outweighed by a deadening familiarity. . . . Less than mesmerized, it struck me that his 'On, somehow on . . . nohow on . . . ' and his 'Only one good, gone, gone for good . . . ' (which I take as meaning that there is both no alternative to, and no point in, proceeding through life) closely resemble to the point of repetition what he has said to me on a string of previous occasions. So now I wonder if it is because of the magic of the man's name that radio allows him to repeat himself to a degree it would not tolerate from other writers.

David Wade, *The Times,* 6 Aug. 1983, p. 5

All Strange Away
Written: 1976, as a variation of the shorter *Imagination Dead Imagine.*
First performed: La Mama Th., New York, 10 Jan. 1984 (dir. Gerald Thomas; with Ryan Cutrona).
Published: London: John Calder, 1979.

'No way in, none out'. In Samuel Beckett's All Strange Away, *a man is caged in a hollow glass rotunda, like a ship model inside a*

bottle, surrounded by mirrored walls and by the sound of his own voice. He is talking himself to death, in this Dantean vision of 'a place to die in', when words ebb, the world ends. Fade to black. . . . It is very much a play and not a reading. . . .

A key to Mr. Thomas's version is in his punctuation of the first three words of the text: 'Imagination dead. Imagine!' In man's extremity, imagination (dreams, reflections, language) is the last resort; it is unimaginable for anyone to exist without it. As with a man drowning, his past life rushes in a whirlpool, and each memory is a momentary anchor . . . Light becomes a catalyst for character, surprising the man and provoking him into speech. When the light dims or shifts its gaze – as in Beckett's *Play* – the man becomes silent. With the help of the actor, the audience is encouraged to use its imagination. When he describes how the cell is closing in on him, the walls of Daniela Thomas's set remain stationary; the actor, in a crouch, mimes his claustrophobia. . . . Some of the additions are enrichments, for example, a moment when the man pinches folds in his garment (long johns) as if trying to pluck mortality.

Mel Gussow, *New York Times,* 11 Jan. 1984, Sec. III, p. 20

b: Fiction

More Pricks than Kicks
Written: in English, 1933.
Published: London: Chatto and Windus, 1934; New York: Grove Press, 1970.

[More Pricks than Kicks *began as* Dream of Fair to Middling Women, *which was never completed.] This odd book . . . consists of nine episodes in the career of a Dublin youth called Belacqua (the tenth episode is devoted to his widow). In them we learn something of his friends, his love affairs, his diversions, his abortive attempt at suicide, and his marriages. Belacqua is a queer creature, a very ineffectual dilettante, much given to introspection and constantly involved in clownish misfortunes. . . . An implicit effect of satire is obtained by embellishing the commonplace with a wealth of observation and sometimes erudition, alternated with sudden brusqueness. Belacqua is more of a theme than a character, an opportunity for the exercise of a picturesque prose style. . . . It is still a very uneven book; but there is a definite, fresh talent at work in it, though it is a talent not yet quite sure of itself.*

> *Times Literary Supplement,* 26 July 1934, p. 526,
> reprinted in *Critical Heritage,* p. 42

Adrift, beset, holding futile conversations with relentless girls whose territory is the physical world, Belacqua is a first sketch for the heroes of Beckett's mature fictions, bumping round in a cosmos where nothing synchronizes or harmonizes. The intended point of the stories is an elaborate pointlessness, a theme for which Beckett at that time did not possess the technique.

> Hugh Kenner, *Reader's Guide,* p. 51

Murphy
Written: in English, 1934-37.
Published: London: Routledge, 1938; Paris: Éditions de minuit, 1947; New York: Grove Press, 1957

It is difficult to give an adequate impression of this book by summarizing its plot or events. One might explain that its hero, Murphy, is an unemployed Irishman in London, who lives on the difference between the cost of his lodgings and the amount he claims for them from his guardian; that his mistress, Celia, is a prostitute who does her best to make him look for work; that his Dublin friend, Neary, loves a girl who loves Murphy, and they spend most of the book looking for him; and that finally, but too late, they track him to an asylum, where he has found a congenial job as attendant. . . . A synopsis of this kind, however, will not suggest the curious flavour of the book except perhaps to those who have read Mr. Beckett's earlier work. . . . It is the author's method which is important, and though it is a method as old as Rabelais, Mr. Beckett's use of it is peculiarly his own. Erudition, violent wit, and a large vocabulary are brought to his analysis of Murphy. . . . The book creates its own world, an elaborate parody of the world we know, yet oddly real.

> *Times Literary Supplement,* 12 Mar. 1938, p. 172,
> reprinted in *Critical Heritage,* p. 45

Murphy, the work of a penniless man just past thirty, may be the first reader-participation novel. Fully to get the hang of it, you must set pieces on the board when you are part way through Chapter II and work out a chess game. You are advised to be vigilant earlier than that. Beckett has greatly enjoyed the game of tucking stray pieces of information into pockets whence only deduction can retrieve them. ... The comedy arises from this, that the novelist employs the language we all employ, a language human beings have devised to conform with the world in which they have been placed. It is odd to find, periodically, that this language, which by its very nature seems adapted to setting forth illusions of the familiar, has lent itself to transcriptions of the impossible, without a ruffled surface, without so much as the equivalent of a lifted eyebrow.

Hugh Kenner, *Reader's Guide,* p. 57-9

The Trilogy: Molloy, Malone Dies, The Unnamable.

Molloy
Written: in French, 1947-49; *translated* into English by Beckett and Patrick Bowles.
Published: Paris: Éditions de minuit, 1951; Paris: Olympia Press; New York: Grove Press, 1955; and in *The Trilogy* (Paris: Olympia Press; London: John Calder, 1960).

Molloy, an old man with one stiff leg and the other stiffening, sets out to find his dying mother, who lives somewhere in a city called X. From as far back as he can remember ... he has been going towards his mother in order to establish their relationship on a less unsettled basis. ... Molloy's wanderings take him first to a city, which may or not be the city X, then to the country, then into a forest. There, no longer able to walk, even with the aid of his crutches, he lies down and begins to crawl, serpent-like, progressing 'fifteen paces a day without exerting [himself] to the limit'. Finally, completely exhausted, he falls into a ditch on the edge of the forest. The second half of the book is a story parallel to Molloy's, which begins at the end and ends at the beginning. Jacques Moran, who leads a tidy life tending his bees and his chickens, receives an order from the messenger Gaber, sent by the invisible Youdi, to go to find Malloy. In company with his son, Moran sets out, knowing that the mission is futile, and that it will lead to the ruin of both himself and his son. Later, having failed to find Molloy, having lost his son somewhere along the way, Moran receives the order from Youdi to return home. He obeys and arrives to find his hives dry, his chickens dead, his house abandoned.

> Richard Seaver, 'Samuel Beckett: an Introduction,' *Merlin,*
> Autumn 1952, p. 76

Beckett settles us in the world of the Nothing where some nothings which are men move about for nothing. The absurdity of the world and the meaninglessness of our condition are conveyed in an absurd and deliberately insignificant fashion; never did anybody dare so openly to insult everything which man holds as certain, up to and including this language which he could at least lean upon to scream his doubt and despair.

> Maurice Nadeau, *Combat,* 12 Apr. 1951,
> trans. Françoise Longhurst in *Critical Heritage,* p. 53

Malone Dies
Written: in French, as *Malone meurt,* 1947-49.
Published: Paris: Éditions de minuit, 1951; New York: Grove
  Press, 1956; London: John Calder, 1958; and in *The Trilogy*
  (Paris: Olympia Press; London: John Calder, 1960).

The narrator, Malone, who says that he imagined the characters of Beckett's previous works, and often confuses his own story with theirs, is going to die. Before his end, he wants to tell himself stories and make an inventory of his 'possessions', in order to pass the time as best as he can. He lies motionless on a miserable bed, in a cell bathed day and night in the same grey light, not really knowing where he is nor who he is. His memories are evanescent, perhaps imaginary. He fails to create stories which 'hold together', confusing the characters and the adventures which happen to them. Is he talking about himself, or are they just creations of his mind? He dies without having managed to elucidate anything: his past life, his present illness, the places where he has lived, the people he met. He was searching for something, but what? Everything, including himself, disappears in an indistinct mist beyond time and space. Even the reality of his approaching death is not certain. Even more rigorously than in Molloy, *Samuel Beckett tries in* Malone Dies *to hunt down an inner being (principle of life?) which escapes all attempts at definition. ... It proclaims the nothingness of life, the nothingness of men; it moves in an absolute nihilism.*

> Maurice Nadeau, *Mercure de France,* March 1952, p. 504
> trans. Françoise Longhurst in *Critical Heritage,* p. 77-8

The Unnamable
Written: in French, as *L'Innommable,* 1949-50.
Published: Paris: Éditions de minuit, 1953; New York: Grove Press, 1958; and in *The Trilogy* (Paris: Olympia Press, 1959; London: John Calder, 1960).

It is true that in The Unnamable *the stories are still trying to survive: the moribund Malone had a bed, a room – Mahood is only a human scrap kept in a jar festooned with Chinese lanterns; and there is also Worm, the unborn, whose existence is nothing but the oppression of his impotence to exist. Several other familiar faces pass, phantoms without substance, empty images mechanically revolving around and empty centre occupied by a nameless 'I'. But now everything has changed, and the experiment, resumed from book to book, achieves its real profundity. There is no longer any question of characters under the reassuring protection of a personal name, no present of an interior monologue: what was narrative has become conflict, what assumed a face, even a face in fragments, is now discountenanced. Who is doing the talking here? Who is this 'I' condemned to speak without respite? ... We might try to say it was the 'author' if this name did not evoke capacity and control, but in any case the man who writes is already no longer Samuel Beckett but the necesssity which has displaced him, ... which has made him a nameless being. The Unnamable, a being without being, who can neither live nor die, neither begin or leave off, the empty site in which an empty voice is raised without effect, masked for better or worse by a porous and agonizing 'I'.*

> Maurice Blanchot, *Nouvelle Revue Francaise,* Oct. 1953,
> p. 678-86, trans. Richard Howard in *Critical Heritage,* p. 119

Watt

Written: in English, 1943-46.
Published: Paris: Olympia Press, 1953; London: Calder and
   Boyars, 1963

The story itself is simple enough. Watt, a gentle, abused and be-mused figure, who moves like a broken doll and dresses like a tramp, arrives at the house of Mr. Knott where he is to replace a servant called Arsene. On his way there he suffers various minor indignities: he first appears ejected angrily from a tram; a railway porter wheeling a milkchurn knocks him over; an eccentric aristo-crat called Lady McCann throws a stone at him; he takes a rest by rolling unhesitatingly into a ditch. Arrived finally at Mr. Knott's, he submits to a long harangue from the departing Arsene, then silently and unquestioningly assumes the duties of ground floor servant, attending to the rituals of the Knott household, which are as elaborate and formalized as those of a Pharaoh. In due course he graduates to the upper floor and the rituals of the bed-room, where he takes the place of Erskine, the senior servant whose time is now up. Finally, his cycle completed, he leaves as silently as he came. When last seen at the railway station he is being abused as usual; the stationmaster knocks him flat and injures him by violently flinging open a door; a bucket of slimy water is emptied over him. But he rises without comment or complaint, mildly requests a ticket to the end of the line, and mildly fades away. It is a beautiful summer morning; all present agree that, for once, it is almost good to be alive. But we already know that Watt's next stop is the lunatic asylum, since the chronological end has already come in the third of the book's four parts. ... He not only moves backwards, his sentence structure, word order, finally the order of the letters in the words have also been turned back to front. His world has become, literally, end on. . . . 'No symbols where none intended' reads the last of the novel's witty addenda. I think we should take the author's word for this, despite a mass of interpretations to the contrary. For what emerges most powerfully from the novel is not any stunning allegory. ... Instead, the subject is total ob-session. In other words, the book is a work of extreme mannerism, a mannerism deliberately pushed to the point of lunacy.

A. Alvarez, *Beckett,* p. 38-9.

83

c: Other Works

Proust. London: Chatto and Windus, 1931.

Poems in English. London: Calder and Boyars, 1961.

Poemes. Paris: Éditions de minuit, 1968.

Collected Poems in English and French. London: John Calder, 1977.

Bing. Paris: Éditions de minuit, 1966.

First Love. Paris: Éditions de minuit, as *Premier amour,* 1970; London: Calder and Boyars, 1973.

For to End Yet Again, and Other Fizzles. London: John Calder. 1976; Paris Éditions de minuit, as *Pour finir encore, et autres foirades,* 1976

Mirlitonnades. Paris: Éditions de minuit, 1978. [35 short poems, written 1976-78.]

One Evening, as *Un Soir,* in *Minuit* No. 37 (Jan. 1980); and in *Journal of Beckett Studies,* No. 6 (Autumn 1980).

Disjecta. London: John Calder, 1983. [Includes Beckett's early critical essays, such as 'Dante . . . Bruno . . . Vico . . . Joyce,' and excerpts from letters.]

From the outset of his career as a writer, Beckett has chosen not to write about his work. As scores of eager scholars and journalists have discovered to their dismay, he has also chosen not to talk about his work, deflecting questions sometimes with humour, other times with annoyance. As he asserted in a letter to Alan Schneider concerning curiosity surrounding *Endgame:* 'I feel the only line is to refuse to be involved in exegesis of any kind. And to insist on the extreme simplicity of dramatic situation and issue. If that's not enough for them, and it obviously isn't, it's plenty for us, and we have no elucidations to offer of mysteries that are all of their making.'

Time after time, journalists report that Beckett asks them whether he is to engage in an interview or a chat; if the latter, then he is congenial and answers impersonal, casual questions. There are a few sources from which we may gather inferences about Beckett's thoughts about his writing. He wrote critical articles on both literature and modern art early in his career, some of which (including 'Three Dialogues', written in 1949 for *Transition*) are conveniently published in *Disjecta.* But these were early in his career, before he had begun writing plays. And the comments are directed not at his own work, but that of others, so any conclusions must necessarily be tentative and limited. The sum total of Beckett's comments about his own writing collected from *Disjecta* is only a handul, and even these are often vague.

Some information can be and has been gathered from Beckett's letters to personal friends and play directors. Dierdre Bair has included in her biography much of Beckett's correspondence with Thomas McGreevy, though her reviewers have harshly criticized her for drawing unwarranted conclusions from Beckett's correspondence. Even in these letters, he seldom elucidates his work at any length, though one can sometimes gather the conditions under which he produced a work.

The most fruitful source of information about Beckett on his own writing comes from accounts of his directing of his own plays. Although he never attends opening-night performances, he has been involved either as director, consultant, or supervisor in most major productions of his drama. He is reported to be absolutely meticulous, though not altogether unbending, in the production of his works, usually going back to the text when there is any question. He is especially exacting about the *sound* of his plays. Actors and directors who have worked with Beckett at length (Donald McWhinnie, Alan Schneider, Roger Blin, Patrick Magee, Billie Whitelaw, Rick Cluchey) develop a respect, loyalty, and personal affection which borders on devotion.

Wherever there are accounts of quoted remarks of Beckett's which illumine particular plays, they have been included among the extracts following each play in Section 2. Some anecdotes have by now become famous – his giving Rick Cluchey his own worn bedroom slippers so that they would sound right in *Krapp's Last Tape,* or his answer to Patrick Magee's query about how (in *Endgame)* he should say that if he could find the key to the cupboard he would kill Hamm: 'Just think that if you could find the key to the cupboard you would kill him'.

What the critic, student, or journalist ultimately comes back to is that conclusions about Beckett's work must emerge from the work itself. Like the characters in Beckett's late plays, the work stands isolated and must speak for itself: 'Hamm as stated, and Clov as stated, *nec tecum nec sine te,* in such a place, and in such a world, that's all I can manage, more than I could'.

Although Beckett himself has provided so few personal comments on his own writing – indeed, partly *because* of this – the critical writing devoted to his works is perhaps the most extensive attracted by any living dramatist. The listing which follows is therefore limited to works published in the English language, and selective even within this limitation. Fuller, or more specialist, bibliographies are provided in many of the full-length studies cited, the most valuable in this respect being those by Robin J. Davis; Martha Fehsenfeld; James T. Tanner and J. Don Vann; and, notably, Raymond Federman and John Fletcher, whose *Samuel Beckett: His Works and His Critics* is the definitive bibliography through 1970.

Full details are provided below of all works cited by short titles in earlier sections.

Full-Length Studies.

Richard L. Admussen, *The Samuel Beckett Manuscripts: a Study.* Boston: G.K. Hall, 1978.

A. Alvarez, *Samuel Beckett.* London: Fontana, 1973.

Dierdre Bair, *Samuel Beckett: a Biography.* London: Jonathan Cape, 1978.

Helene L. Baldwin, *Samuel Beckett's Real Silence.* Univ. Park: Pennsylvania State University Press, 1981.

Beckett at 60: a Festschrift. London: Calder and Boyars, 1967.

Morris Beja, S.E. Gontarski, and Pierre Astier, *Samuel Beckett: Humanistic Perspectives.* Ohio State University Press, 1982. [Collection of critical essays.]

Guy Christian Bernard, *Samuel Beckett: a New Approach. A Study of the Novels and Plays.* London: Dent; New York: Dodd, Mead, 1970.

Tom Bishop and Raymond Federman, eds., *Samuel Beckett.* Paris: L'Herne, 1977.

Frederick Busi, *The Transformation of Godot.* Lexington: University of Kentucky, 1980.

John Calder, ed., *A Samuel Beckett Reader.* London: Calder and Boyars, 1967.

Bell G. Chevigny, ed., *Twentieth Century Interpretations of Endgame.* Englewood Cliffs, New Jersey: Prentice-Hall, 1969.

Richard N. Coe, *Beckett.* Edinburgh; London: Oliver and Boyd, 1964.

Ruby Cohn, *Back to Beckett.* Princeton, New Jersey:
Princeton University Press, 1974.
—————, ed., *Casebook on Waiting for Godot.* New York: Grove
Press, 1967.
—————, *Just Play: Beckett's Theater.* Princeton, N.J.: Princeton
University Press, 1980.
—————, ed., *Samuel Beckett: a Collection of Criticism.* New
York: McGraw-Hill, 1975.
—————, *Samuel Beckett: the Comic Gamut.* New Brunswick,
New Jersey: Rutgers University Press, 1962.
Hannah C. Copeland, *Art and the Artist in the Works of Samuel
Beckett.* The Hague: Mouton, 1975.
Ramona Cormier and Janis L. Pallister, *Waiting for Death: the
Philosophical Significance of En Attendant Godot.*
Montgomery: University of Alabama Press, 1977.
Robin J. Davis, *Samuel Beckett: Checklist and Index of his
Published Works 1967-1976.* University of Stirling, 1979.
Francis M. Doherty, *Samuel Beckett.* London: Hutchinson, 1971.
Colin Duckworth, *Angels of Darkness: Dramatic Effect in Samuel
Beckett with Special Reference to Eugene Ionesco.* London:
Allen and Unwin, 1972.
James Eliopulos, *Samuel Beckett's Dramatic Language.* The
Hague: Mouton, 1975.
Martin Esslin, ed., *Samuel Beckett: a Collection of Critical Essays.*
Englewood Cliffs, New Jersey: Prentice-Hall, 1965.
Raymond Federman and John Fletcher, *Samuel Beckett: His
Works and his Critics: an Essay in Bibliography.* Berkeley,
Los Angeles, London: University of California Press, 1970.
Martha Fehsenfeld, *The Samuel Beckett Collection: a Catalogue.*
Univ. of Reading: The Library, 1979.
Beryl S. Fletcher, John Fletcher, Barry Smith, and Walter Bachen,
A Student's Guide to the Plays of Samuel Beckett. London
and Boston: Faber and Faber, 1978.
John Fletcher and John Spurling, *Beckett: a Study of His Plays.*
London: Methuen; New York: Hill and Wang, 1972.
John Fletcher, *Samuel Beckett's Art.* London: Chatto and
Windus, 1967.
John Fletcher, *The Novels of Samuel Beckett.* London: Chatto
and Windus, 1964.
Melvin J. Friedman, *Samuel Beckett Now: Critical Approaches to
His Novels, Poetry and Plays.* Chicago: University of Chicago
Press, 1970.
Barbara Gluck, *Beckett and Joyce: Friendship and Fiction.*
Lewisburg: Bucknell University Press, 1979.

S. Gontarski, *Beckett's Happy Days: an Analysis of the Manuscript.* Athens: Ohio State University Press, 1977.

Alice and Kenneth Hamilton, *Condemned to Life: the World of Samuel Beckett.* Grand Rapids, Mich.: Eardmans, 1976.

Per Olof Hagberg, *The Dramatic Works of Samuel Beckett and Harold Pinter: a Comparative Analysis of Main Themes and Dramatic Technique.* Gotenborg: University of Göthenburg, 1972.

Lawrence E. Harvey, *Samuel Beckett: Poet and Critic.* Princeton, New Jersey: Princeton University Press, 1970.

Ihab Hassan, *The Literature of Silence: Henry Miller and Samuel Beckett.* New York: Knopf, 1967.

Ronald Hayman, *Samuel Beckett.* London: Heinemann, 1970.

Georg Hensel, *Beckett.* Hannover: Freidrich Verlag, 1968. [Illustrations of German productions.]

David H. Hesla, *The Shape of Chaos: an Interpretation of the Art of Samuel Beckett.* St. Paul: University of Minnesota Press, 1971.

Frederick J. Hoffman, *Samuel Beckett: the Language of Self.* Carbondale: Southern Illinois University Press, 1962. [Also published under the title *Samuel Beckett: the Man and His Works* (Toronto: Forum House, 1969).]

Josephine Jacobson and William R. Mueller, *The Testament of Samuel Beckett.* New York: Hill and Wang, 1964; London: Faber and Faber, 1966.

Hugh Kenner, *A Reader's Guide to Samuel Beckett.* New York: Farrar, Straus and Giroux, 1973.

———, *Samuel Beckett: a Critical Study.* New York: Grove Press, 1961; London: John Calder, 1962. Rev. ed., Los Angeles: University of California Press, 1968.

James Knowlson, *Light and Darkness in the Theatre of Samuel Beckett.* London: Turret Books, 1972.

———, *Samuel Beckett: an Exhibition held at Reading University Library, May to July, 1971.* London: Turret Books, 1971.

——— and John Pilling, *Frescoes of the Skull.* London: Calder, 1977.

———, ed., *Krapp's Last Tape. (Theatre Workbook I.)* London: Brutus Books, 1980. [Includes reviews and interviews with directors and actors.]

Eric P. Levy, *Beckett and the Voice of Species.* London: Gill and Macmillan, 1980.

J.P. Little, *Beckett: En Attendant Godot and Fin de Partie.* London: Grant and Cutler, 1981 [Critical guide to French texts].

Charles R. Lyons, *Samuel Beckett.* New York: Macmillan, 1983.

Jean I. Mayoux, *Samuel Beckett.* Harlow: Longman, for the British Council, 1974.

Vivian Mercier, *Beckett-Beckett: the Truth of Contradictions.* New York: Oxford University Press, 1977.

Kristin C. Morrison, *Centers and Chronicles: the Use of Narrative in the Plays of Samuel Beckett and Harold Pinter.* London and Chicago: University of Chicago Press, 1983.

Patrick Murray, *The Tragic Comedian: a Study of Samuel Beckett.* Cork: Mercier Press, 1970.

John Pilling, *Samuel Beckett.* London: Routledge, 1976.

Alex Reid, *All I Can Manage, More Than I Could: an Approach to the Plays of Samuel Beckett.* Dublin: Dolmen Press, 1968.

Micheal Robinson, *The Long Sonata of the Dead: a Study of Samuel Beckett.* London: Hart-Davis, 1969.

Steven J. Rosen, *Samuel Beckett and the Pessimistic Tradition.* New Brunswick, New Jersey: Rutgers University Press, 1976.

Nathan A. Scott, *Samuel Beckett.* London: Bowes and Bowes, 1965.

Yasunari Takahashi, *Samuel Beckett.* Tokyo: Kenkyusha, 1971.

James T. Tanner and J. Don Vann, *Samuel Beckett: A Checklist of Criticism.* Ohio: Kent State University Press, 1969.

William York Tindall, *Beckett's Bums.* London: Shenval Press, 1960.

_____, *Samuel Beckett.* New York and London: Columbia University Press, 1964.

Eugene Webb, *Samuel Beckett.* Seattle: University of Washington Press, 1970.

Katherine Worth, ed., *Beckett the Shape Changer: a Symposium.* London: Routledge, 1975.

Clas Zilliacus, *Beckett and Broadcasting: a Study of the Works of Samuel Beckett for and in Radio and Television* (Acts Academiae Aboensis, Ser. A, Vol. LI, No. 2). Abo: Abo Akademi, 1976.

Articles and Chapters in Books

J. Acheson, 'Chess with the Audience: Samuel Beckett's *Endgame',* *Critical Quarterly,* XXII (Summer 1980), p. 33-45.

Robert Martin Adams, *Afterjoyce* (New York: Oxford University Press, 1977), p. 90-113.

Richard L. Admussen, 'Samuel Beckett's Unpublished Writings', *Journal of Beckett Studies,* No. 1 (Winter 1976), p. 66-74.

David Alpaugh, *'Embers* and the Sea: Beckettian Intimations of Mortality', *Modern Drama,* XVI (March 1973), p. 317-28.
_____, 'The Symbolic Structure of Samuel Beckett's *All That Fall', Modern Drama,* IX (December 1966), p. 324-32.

Walter D. Asmus, 'Practical Aspects of Theatre, Radio and Television: Rehearsal Notes for the German Premiere of Beckett's *That Time* and *Footfalls* at the Schiller-Theatre Werkstatt, Berlin', *Journal of Beckett Studies,* No. 2 (Summer 1977), p. 82-95.

Pierre Astier, 'Beckett's *Ohio Impromptu:* a View from the Isle of Swans', *Modern Drama,* XXV (1982), p. 331-41.

Michael Beausang, 'Myth and Tragi-Comedy in Beckett's *Happy Days', Mosaic,* V (1971), p. 59-78.

'Beckett and the Literature of Ruin', *Chicago Review,* XXXIII, 2 (1982), p. 79-106 [Symposium.]

Mary Benson, 'Blin on Beckett', *Theatre,* X, 1 (Fall 1978), p. 90-3. [Interview on directing and acting].

Linda Ben-Zvi, 'The Schizmatic Self in *A Piece of Monologue', Journal of Beckett Studies,* No. 7 (Spring 1982), p. 7-18.

Albert Bermel, *Contradictory Characters: an Interpretation of the Modern Theatre* (New York: Dutton, 1973), p. 159-84.

Herbert Blau, *The Impossible Theater: a Manifesto* (New York: Macmillan; London: Collier Macmillan, 1964), p. 221-51.

Enoch Brater, 'The "Absurd" Actor in the Theatre of Samuel Beckett', *Educational Theatre Journal,* XXVII (May 1975), p. 197-207.
_____, 'Brecht's Alienated Actor in Beckett's Theatre', *Comparative Drama,* IX, iii (Fall 1975), p. 195-205.
_____, 'Dada, Surrealism, and the Genesis of *Not I', Modern Drama,* XVIII (1975), p. 49-59.
_____, 'Fragment and Beckett's Form in *That Time* and *Footfalls', Journal of Beckett Studies,* No. 2 (Summer 1977), p. 70-81.
_____, 'The "I" in Beckett's *Not I', Twentieth Century Literature,* XX (July 1974), p. 189-200.
_____, 'Light, Sound, Movement, and Action in Beckett's *Rockaby', Modern Drama,* XXV (1982), p. 342-8.
_____, 'Thinking Eye in Beckett's *Film', Modern Language Quarterly,* XXXVI (June 1975), p. 166-76.

Rolf Breur, 'The Solution as Problem: Beckett's *Waiting for Godot', Modern Drama,* XIX (1976), p. 225-36.

A.W. Brink, 'Universality in Samuel Beckett's *Endgame', Queen's Quarterly,* LXXVIII (Summer 1971), p. 191-207.

Peter Brook, *'Endgame* as King Lear, or How to Stop Worrying and Love Beckett', *Encore,* XII (January-February 1965), p. 8-12.

John Russell Brown, 'Dialogue in Pinter and Others', *Critical Quarterly,* VII (Autumn 1965), p. 225-43.

———, 'Mr. Beckett's Shakespeare', *Critical Quarterly,* V (Winter 1963), p. 310-26.

Robert Brustein, *Seasons of Discontent: Dramatic Opinions 1959-1965* (New York: Simon and Schuster, 1965; London: Jonathan Cape, 1966), p. 24-8; 53-6; 182-4; 202-3.

Peter Bull, *I Know the Face, But* . . . (London: Peter Davies, 1959), p. 166-91. [On playing Pozzo.]

S. Campbell, *'Krapp's Last Tape* and Critical Theory', *Comparative Drama,* XII (Fall 1978), p. 187-99.

Pierre Chabert, 'Beckett as Director,' *Gambit,* No. 28 (1976) p. 41-63.

———, 'The Body in Beckett's Theatre', *Journal of Beckett Studies,* No. 8 (Autumn 1982), p. 23-9.

Louise Cleveland, 'Trials in Soundscape: the Radio Plays of Beckett', *Modern Drama,* XI (1968), p. 267-82.

Rick Cluchey, 'My Years with Beckett', *New Edinburgh Review,* No. 51 (Aug. 1980), p. 18-21.

Ruby Cohn, 'Beckett Books of the 1970s', *Educational Theatre Journal,* XXV (May 1973), p. 243-51.

———, 'Outward Bound Soliloquies', *Journal of Modern Literature,* VI (February 1977), p. 17-38.

———, 'Shakespearian Embers in Beckett', *Modern Shakespeare Offshoots* (Princeton, New Jersey: Princeton University Press, 1976), p. 375-88.

P.H. Collins, 'Proust, Time, and Beckett's *Happy Days'*, *French Review,* Special Issue VI (1974), p. 105-19.

Ethel F. Cornwall, 'Samuel Beckett: the Flight from Self', *PMLA,* LXXXVIII (1973), p. 41-51.

Richard S. Dietrich, 'Beckett's Goad: From Stage to Film', *Literature/Film Quarterly,* IV (Winter 1976), p. 83-9. [On film of *Act Without Words II.*]

Livio Dobrez, 'Beckett, Sartre and Camus: the Darkness and the Light', *Southern Review* VII (July 1974), p. 51-63.

Tom F. Driver, 'Beckett by the Madeleine', *Columbia University Forum,* IV (Summer 1961). [Interview].

Bernard Dukore and Daniel Gerould, *Avant-Garde Drama: a Casebook* (London: Crowell, 1975).

Martin Esslin, 'Samuel Beckett and the Art of Broadcasting', *Encounter,* XLV (September 1975), p. 38-46.

_____, 'Voices, Patterns, Voices: Samuel Beckett's Later Plays', *Gambit,* No. 28 (1976), p. 93-9.

_____, *The Theatre of the Absurd,* revised ed. (Garden City, New York: Doubleday, 1969), p. 11-65.

Raymond Federman, 'Samuel Beckett's Film on the Agony of Perceivedness', *James Joyce Quarterly,* VIII (1971), p. 363-71.

Martha Fehsenfeld, 'Beckett's Late Works: an Appraisal', *Modern Drama,* XXV (1982), p. 331-41.

Ernst Fischer, 'Samuel Beckett: *Play* and *Film',* *Mosaic,* II, ii (1969), p. 96-116.

John Fletcher, 'Roger Blin at Work', *Modern Drama,* VIII (1966), p. 403-8.

W.J. Free, 'Beckett's Plays and the Photographic Vision', *Georgia Review,* XXXIV (Winter 1980), p. 801-12.

Melvin Friedman, 'Review-Essay: Samuel Beckett and His Critics Enter the 1970s', *Studies in the Novel,* V (1973), p. 383-99.

Ronald Gaskell, *Drama and Reality: the European Theatre since Ibsen* (London: Routledge, 1972), p. 147-56.

Richard Gilman, 'Beckett', *Partisan Review,* XLI (1974), p. 56-76.

_____, *The Making of Modern Drama: a Study of Büchner, Ibsen, Strindberg, Chekhov, Pirandello, Brecht, Handke* (New York: Farrar, Straus, Giroux, 1974), p. 234-66.

S. Golden, 'Familiars in a Ruinstrewn Land: *Endgame* as Political Allegory', *Contemporary Literature,* XXII (Fall 1981), p. 425-55

Stanley E. Gontarski, *'Krapp's First Tape:* Beckett's Manuscript', *Journal of Modern Literature,* VI (February 1977), p. 61-8.

_____, 'The Anatomy of Beckett's *Eh Joe',* *Modern Drama,* XXVI (1982), p. 425-34.

_____, 'Making Yourself All Up Again; the Composition of Samuel Beckett's *That Time',* *Modern Drama,* XXIII (1980), p. 112-20.

Randolph Goodman, ed., 'The Old Tune', *From Script to Stage* (San Francisco: Rinehart, 1971), p. 540-74. [Documentation and interviews.]

John Goodwin, ed., *Peter Hall's Diaries* (London: Hamilton, 1983).

David I. Grossvogel, *Four Playwrights and a Postcript: Brecht, Ionesco, Genet* (Ithaca: Cornell University Press, 1962), p. 85-131.

Stephen M. Halloran, 'The Anti-Aesthetics of *Waiting for Godot',* *Centennial Review,* XVI (Winter 1972), p. 69-81.

Ihab Hassan, *The Dismemberment of Orpheus: Toward a Post-modern Literature* (New York: Oxford University Press, 1971), p. 210-50.

_____, 'Joyce, Beckett and the Postmodern Imagination', *Triquarterly,* No. 34 (Fall 1975), p. 179-200.

David Hayman, 'A Coming of Age: Beckett Biblioglorified', *James Joyce Quarterly,* VIII (1971), p. 413-20.

Sylvie Debevec Henning, *'Film:* a Dialogue between Beckett and Berkeley', *Journal of Beckett Studies,* No. 7 (Spring 1982), p. 89-100.

_____, 'Samuel Beckett's *Film* and *La Derniere Bande:* Intra-textual and Intertextual Daubles', *Symposium,* XXXV (Summer 1981), p. 131-53.

William Hutt and R. O'Driscoll, *'Waiting for Godot',* in Peter Raby, ed., *The Stratford Scene, Toronto* (1968), p. 230-41.

H. Kayssar, 'Theatre Games, Language Games and *Endgame', Theatre Journal,* XXXI (May 1979), p. 221-38.

Katherine Kelly, 'The Orphic Mouth in *Not I', Journal of Beckett Studies,* No. 6 (Autumn 1980), p. 73-80.

Andrew K. Kennedy, *Six Dramatists in Search of a Language: Studies in Dramatic Language* (Cambridge: Cambridge University Press, 1975), p. 130-64.

Edith Kern, 'Beckett and the Spirit of the Commedia Dell'Arte,' *Modern Drama,* IX (1966), p. 260-7.

James Knowlson, 'Beckett and John Millington Synge', *Gambit,* No. 28 (1976), p. 65-81.

_____, *'Krapp's Last Tape:* the Evolution of a Play', *Journal of Beckett Studies,* I (Winter 1976), p. 50-65.

Paul Lawley, 'Counterpoint, Absence, and the Medium in Beckett's *Not I', Modern Drama,* XXVI (1983), p. 407-14.

_____, *'Embers:* an Interpretation', *Journal of Beckett Studies,* No. 6 (Autumn 1980), p. 9-36.

_____, 'Symbolic Structure and Creative Obligation in *Endgame', Journal of Beckett Studies,* No. 5 (Autumn 1979), p. 45-66.

Antoni Libera, 'Structure and Pattern in *That Time', Journal of Beckett Studies,* No. 6 (Autumn 1980), p. 81-90.

Jane Lyman, ed., 'Beckett: *Waiting for Godot', Perspectives on Plays* (London: Routledge, 1976), p. 257-73. [Excerpts from Jack MacGowran, Sean O'Casey, Martin Esslin, Alain Robbe-Grillet.]

Charles R. Lyons, 'Beckett's Major Plays and the Trilogy', *Comparative Drama,* V (Winter 1971-72), p. 254-68.

_____, 'Perceiving *Rockaby* — as a Text, as a Text by Samuel Beckett, as a Text for Performance', *Comparative Drama,* Winter 1982-83, p. 297-311.

Frederick J. Marker, 'Beckett Criticism in *Modern Drama:* a Checklist', *Modern Drama,* XIX (1976), p. 261-3.

Jean-Jacques Mayoux, 'Samuel Beckett and the Mass Media', in Bernard Harris, ed., *Essays and Studies 1971* (Humanities Press, 1971), p. 83-100.

James Mays, 'Samuel Beckett Bibliography: Comments and Corrections', *Irish University Review,* II, ii (Autumn 1972), p. 189-208.

Donald McWhinnie, *The Art of Radio* (London: Faber and Faber, 1959).

B. Mitchell, 'Beckett Bibliography: New Works, 1976-1982', *Modern Fiction Studies,* XXIX (Spring 1983), p. 131-52.

Kristin Morrison, 'Defeated Sexuality in the Plays and Novels of Samuel Beckett', *Comparative Drama,* XIV (Spring 1980), p. 18-34.

_____ , 'The Rip Word in *A Piece of Monologue',* *Modern Drama,* XXV(1982), p. 331-41.

Benedict Nightingale, *An Introduction of Fifty Modern Plays* (London: Pan, 1982), p. 258-84. [*Godot; Endgame, Not I.*]

Joseph O'Neill, 'The Absurd in Samuel Beckett', *Personalist,* XLVII (1967), p. 56-76.

Ruth Perlmutter, 'Beckett's *Film* and Beckett and Film', *Journal of Modern Literature,* VI (February 1977), p. 83-94.

T. Postlewait, 'Self Performing Voices: Mind, Memory, and Time in Beckett's Drama', *Twentieth Century Literature,* XXIV (Winter 1978), p. 473-91.

Rosemary Pountney, 'On Acting Mouth in *Not I', Journal of Beckett Studies,* No. 1 (Winter 1970), p. 81-5.

Leonard C. Pronko, *Avant-Garde: the Experimental Theatre in France* (Berkeley and Los Angeles: University of California Press; London: Cambridge University Press, 1962), p. 22-58.

David Read, 'Artistic Theory in the Work of Samuel Beckett', *Journal of Beckett Studies,* No. 9 (Autumn 1982), p. 7-22.

C.J.B. Robinson, 'A Way with Words: Paradox, Silence, and Samuel Beckett', *Cambridge Quarterly,* V (1971), p. 249-64.

Carol Rosen, *Plays of Impasse: Contemporary Drama Set in Confining Institutions* (Princeton University Press, 1983).

Alan Schneider, ' "Any Way You Like, Alan"; Working with Beckett', *Theatre Quarterly,* No. 19 (1975), p. 27-38.

R.K. Simon, 'Dialectical Laughter: a Study of *Endgame', Modern Drama,* XXV (1982), p. 505-13.

Thomas R. Simone, ' "Faint, though by no means invisible": a Commentary on Beckett's *Footfalls', Modern Drama,* XXVI (1983), p. 435-46.

95

Alan Simpson, *Beckett and Behan, and a Theatre in Dublin*
(London: Routledge, 1962), p. 62-138.

Patrick Starnes, 'Samuel Beckett: an Interview', *Antigonish
Review,* X (Summer 1972), p. 49-53.

Darko Suvin, 'Beckett's Purgatory of the Individual, or the Three
Laws of Thermodynamics', *Drama Review,* II, iv (Summer
1967), p. 23-36.

George H. Szanto, 'Samuel Beckett: Dramatic Possibilities',
Massachusetts Review, XV (Autumn 1974), p. 735-61.

R. Torrance, 'Modes of Being and Time in the World of Godot',
Modern Language Quarterly, XXVIII (1967), p. 77-95.

Richard Toscan, 'MacGowran on Beckett', *Theatre Quarterly,*
No. 11 (1973), p. 217-28.

Simon Trussler, *'Happy Days:* Two Productions and a Text',
Prompt, No. 4 (1964), p. 23-5.

Kenneth Tynan, *Curtains* (London: Longmans; New York:
Atheneum, 1961), p. 101-3; 225-8; 272; 401-3.

Aspasia Velissariou, 'Language in *Waiting for Godot', Journal of
Beckett Studies,* No. 8 (Autumn 1982), p. 45-58.

George Wellwarth, *The Theater of Protest and Paradox* (New
York: New York University Press, revised ed. 1971), p. 41-56.

Keith Whitlock, *The Varied Scene* (London: Oxford University
Press, 1977), p. 9-28.

Thomas R. Whittaker, 'Notes on Playing the Player', *Centennial
Review,* XVI (Winter 1972), p. 1-22.

Robert Wilcher, 'What's It Mean to Mean? An Approach to
Beckett's Theatre', *Critical Quarterly,* XVIII (Summer 1976),
p. 9-37.

Daniel Wolf and Edwin Fancer, eds., *The Village Voice Reader:
a Mixed Bag from the Greenwich Village Newspaper* (Garden
City: Doubleday, 1962). [Separate reviews.]

Katherine J. Worth, 'Audio-Visual Beckett', *Journal of Beckett
Studies,* No. 1 (Winter 1976), p. 85-8.

――――, 'Beckett and the Radio Medium', in *British Radio
Drama,* ed. John Drakakis (London: Cambridge University
Press, 1981), p. 191-217.

William B. Worthen, 'Beckett's Actor', *Modern Drama,* XXVI
(1983), p. 415-24.

Hersh Zeifman, 'Being and Non-Being: Samuel Beckett's *Not I',
Modern Drama,* XIX (1976), p. 35-46.